The Native American Herbalism and Essential Oils Encyclopedia

2 Books in 1: The Native American Herbalism Encyclopedia, Complete Medical Herbs Handbook – The Complete Book of Essential Oils

Contents

The Native American Herbalism Encyclopedia

The Complete Beginner's Guide to Native American Medicinal Herbs and Natural Remedies

Dr. Christina Zielinski

Chapter 1: Introduction

It's a significant part of alternative medicine, also is beneficial in treating and preventing numerous common ailments. Nature's pharmacy is extensive, full of herbs that have potent medicinal properties. With knowledge and guidance, everybody can utilize herbs to alleviate discomfort and promote healing. Growing up in the hills of Montana, I'd hear stories about Native Americans cured all sorts of ailments using treatments made with a number of the wild plants that grew only outside our family. Today I delight in developing plenty of aromatic herbs in my backyard and at the hardwood woods behind my property. On these infrequent occasions when I am not feeling well, I'm often able to look after myself using plants I have chosen and ready. Some herbal remedies involve utilizing plant components in their new, natural condition. By conducting a little research, making sure that a particular herb is safe and right for me, and adhering to any related precautions, I have managed to care for my health and cure minor ailments until they worsen require medical intervention. While it was challenging to buy medicinal herbs, it's now quite simple to discover the most well-known ones in high-street shops and even on the shelves of big-box shops. Health food stores offer you an extensive choice of complete herbs, together with tinctures, powders, teas, and other products, which make it easy to bypass pharmaceuticals. It could come as a surprise to find out that quite a few traditional pills have their roots firmly implanted in herbal medicine. Quinine, an essential medication for treating malaria, comes out of the cinchona tree's bark, and digoxin, a powerful drug used in cardiac circumstances, comes in the beautiful but poisonous foxglove.

- Many different pharmaceuticals are plant-established or synthesized using chemicals that are equal to those found in nature. However, mainstream medicine prefers synthetic drugs due to their standardization, innocence, and simplicity of usage. Understandably, prescription pharmaceuticals have made a coveted position. It's not the aim of the publication to downplay their significance. But it is just as important to keep in mind that herbs are regarded as dietary supplements in the USA. If marketed commercially, they are controlled as such. Thus, whenever you choose to treat a disease the pure manner, you do not need to acquire a prescription--since you would be using a synthetic medication --to use an herbal poultice, employ a straightforward cream or petroleum, or have a tincture or tea.

- While herbs are healthy, most don't possess the unwanted effects which often accompany medication. They don't inhibit the body's normal recovery process; instead, they improve our capacity to recover, especially when paired with the remainder. Many herbs help enhance the immune system, making it much easier for the body to utilize its natural defenses against infections and viruses.

- Cataloging the planet's medicinal plants could require a massive effort, and, even then, it would be almost impossible to cover each of the properties provided by each plant. When there are lots of excellent and comprehensive manuals detailing hundreds of herbs, it can be hard to determine what to use--particularly when there are many alternatives to choose from. You will get a guide to utilizing some of the planet's most common and potent medicinal herbs. They all are simple to locate on the internet or in the regional health food shop.

Additionally, it is quite probable you could discover some of them growing inside a brief space of your front door. Some might even be hiding within your spice cupboard! Whether you're a newcomer to this world of herbal medication or have begun experiencing the healing power of plants, then you will find this publication helpful. The principal section of this book covers 75 ordinary disorders, together with remedies for each. The last chapter comprises 40 herbaceous plants' profiles, such as significant notes and precautions for identifying and expanding them if you prefer. As you may be interested in the curative power of plant-based medications and goods, perhaps you're reluctant to dip a toe into those ethereal waters. However, you don't need to quite over-the-counter medication to get on board using herbal remedies.

A massive stack of supplements clarifies that whoever eats the maximum vegetables wins a concerning diet. One motive herbalism could be so successful as preventative and curative medicine is since, in many situations, the herbs we utilize today as medication are plants that were considered "vegetables" through all human history. So often today, the kinds of disorders we see are because of a deficiency of essential nutrients. On the Most Elementary level, herbs may help us fill in such gaps and maintain our bodies moving strong

In most likelihood, herbs are already part of your self-medication or beautification regular --you simply don't realize it. Look carefully at the ingredient listing on several facial lotions and cleansers, shampoos and sprays, and even cough drops. You will probably discover herbal extracts of lots of the ingredients dealt with inside this publication. Frequent problems we confront every day--out of acne, dry skin, or brittle hair to fatigue, mild depression, or anxiety --may be averted, diminished, or treated via the targeted use of herb-infused creams, shampoos, teas, and much more. You might have discovered that herbal medicine does not work. It is not rooted in mathematics, or it is based on historical principles that are not applicable in a contemporary world. The truth is, there is a motive that herbs (and meals) are used to cure, restore, and protect people from injuries and illness for centuries. Start to comprehend it by researching these common phrases often tossed about such as organic salad greens: Essential oils have been contradictory volatile oils extracted from portions of a plant, such as stalks, leaves, blossoms, and fruits, which provide away a particular healing odor. Antioxidants are compounds found in herbs, plants, and food, plus they fight the damaging oxidizing agents which destroy cells.

Antioxidants are required to fix or protect against cell damage and reduce your odds of disease. Vitamins are chemicals that your body gets from food to execute certain functions it can't perform by itself. Essential oils, vitamins, antioxidants, and other curing compounds activate our bodies to operate effectively, strengthen our immunity, and combat illness all around. Herbal preparations offer you the vehicles for all these healing agents to come in contact with our bodies. You are likely aware that many of these materials are extracted and analyzed by scientists, re-engineered in labs, and made accessible in pharmaceutical medications. By studying this book and garnish with all the recipes, you can get closer to the origin of things--that the bit of this equation comes before meds and reengineering. In these pages, you're going to get the right talk about the very strongly healing herbs (with no brand pushes, business affiliations (or philosophical agendas), and the reason why they work and how to integrate them in a modern home. By taking more of a complementary approach to beauty and health, your physician's visits may begin to be fewer and further between. The attention of medicinal usage has changed from herbal medications to artificial drugs in the previous century. There's a motion to rethink the advantages of herbal medications. There's a school advocating the use of conventional medicine along with some more western kind of treatment. Herbal medications are, nevertheless, in contrast to common belief, not resistant to adverse results. Thus physicians, pharmacists and other caregivers, in addition to patients themselves, want to expand their understanding of herbal medications.

Patients are always taught how to look after their health. Since quite a few herbal medications are used in self-maintenance, a larger awareness of the advantages and the potential unwanted effects is required. A fantastic glimpse into the islands demonstrates that possibly harmful reactions can result from the utilization of these medications since many consider herbal treatment presents a chance of causing injury. On the one hand, insufficient knowledge about the topic not just by individuals but also by some caregivers may explain negative consequences. On the other hand, misconceptions regarding herbal medications may restrict the number of patients who might benefit from their usage. Simple accessibility to patients makes the neighborhood pharmacists the perfect healthcare professionals for supplying the essential info and guidance. Pharmacies benefit from being conveniently found along with the community pharmacist is readily available and might be approached without needing a previous appointment. This publication on herbal medications intends to supply enough info to excite the reader's attention for additional reading. Hence the referenced character of the work. Like so many other housewives of this day, she was anticipated to be the family physician, should need be. Making powerful, gentle medication generally was not a complex affair. When a baby had colic, you fed him a small hot catnip, Chamomile, or calendula tea and then bathed him at a linden blossom or catnip tea tub. If you had a terrible cough, then you could earn a fine soothing medication from honey, powerful black cherry berry tea, and actual apple cider vinegar. Together with her many kids, my great-grandmother researched the hollows and mountains of Deadly Appalachia, learning how to recognize the local flora and fauna, and gathered beneficial herbs to use as therapeutic drugs. I never intended to get an herbalist, a fan of the plant kingdom, a founder of curing formulas. I believe that it was -- and is my fate. We wanted to walk and research together with my grandfather because he did his actions. On one specific walk, my grandfather and I had been drifting through cattle pastures and forests -- his large, rough predator hand holding my tender little woman hand -- and that I will remember him telling me, "Where we grew up, we did not go to physicians unless it was a dire crisis. We did not have enough money.

Our mom made medication from the regional herbs she dosed us if we liked it or not. The stuff you needed to consume often did not taste great. The medications that have rubbed into your skin, such as the herbal salves, garnished with neighborhood beeswax, lard, or lanolin, along with also the brownish-green colored liniments created with homemade strawberry wine or corn whiskey, were utilized to stop infections, alleviate stuffiness, help you sleep, or even create your muscles feel much better after a long day on the job. Those things worked nice and many times smelled pretty great, also." I had been curious. So started my "training" He taught me that the titles of their trees and the green crops, the uses and medicinal qualities of bark my "training, acorns, pine sap, roots, leaves, blossoms, as well as the grey-blue clay at the stream banks. I can recall my fourth-grade science instructor being astonished at just how much I understood! I discovered these free-for-the-taking "medications of the ground" could help the body's natural methods to cure ailments within and without. I fell in love with the thought that nature could supply nearly anything you had to take care of your well-being and beauty naturally.

Today, as a certified holistic aesthetician, certified aromatherapist, and neighborhood herbalist, I dedicate my career to plant-based topical nutritional supplements and supplements for skin ailments. I compose, invent treatments, increase herbs, instruct, and function as an herbal practitioner. I believe that my grandfather's soul has pushed me to spread the word about herbs' healing benefits. This publication represents the group of topical herbal curing formulations that, within the previous 30 years, I have grown, experimented with, and perfected into the top of my skill. In these pages, I will share my comments, understanding, and observations with you, based on collective wisdom and experience, of how our green neighbors, the blossoms, may be powerful medication. I hope you find the instructions simple to follow along with the treatments useful, finding the directions simple to follow, and the treatments useful, together with the ideal lifestyle and diet. They could bring substantial relief to ordinary skin ailments and body disorders and improve your well-being and relaxation!

1.1 History of Herbal Medicine

Odds are you have heard of Ginkgo Biloba, even if you don't understand much--of anything about it. This plant includes antioxidants called flavonoids, which are utilized to enhance cognitive functions. But did you realize that scientists discovered fossilized ginkgo Bilboa's relationship to the pre-dinosaur era (about 270 million years ago)? In Western herbalism, there will also be recorded records of early Egyptians with garlic to prevent and cure illness, boost strength; and juniper oil to handle bladder and kidney diseases. These findings return to 1700 BCE. From 100 BCE, the Greeks established a thorough methodology that attached different herbs to seasons and fire, air, ground, and water elements. In 77 CE, a Greek physician called Padania's Discords catalogued over 600 plants and their recovery applications. The Romans afterwards added the Greek philosophies and a cataloging system that's still utilized in medicine today. One case of that is that the Hindu focus on prevention instead of remedies. Herbal remedies can also be found in ancient Eastern medicine traditions like Traditional Chinese Medicine (TCM) and Ayurveda. Australian aborigines, by way of instance, found tea tree oil, a highly effective antiseptic. Many healing herbs are located in South American rain forests and hills. Ancient cultures additionally used herbs for decorative purposes. In 1500 BCE, Egyptians recorded using various herbs. Ancient Greeks used climbed waters and oils to cleanse and moisturize skin. The very same sorts of remedies are still quite common today.

Do you need shinier hair or even a dandruff-free scalp? A nettle-based tonic is going to do just fine. No nettles? No issue. Parsley and rosemary operate, also. Want more luminous skin? Place a couple of drops of peppermint oil on your moisturizer to kill surface bacteria and improve blood circulation. Or, incorporate rosemary in your regimen. It regulates oil production to be the greatest acne fighter; its calming effects work wonders for women experiencing menopause. Contemporary medicine is much more targeted and complicated." But, plant-based substances are employed in many modern pharmaceuticals. In other words, crops are natural healers. That fact has not changed since the start of time. It has only evolved over generations since it is merged with contemporary delivery systems and technological tools.

Before pharmaceutical businesses fabricated drugs, people treated their disorders using exactly what the ground supplied. Herbal medicine isn't new, whether that was an intuitive procedure or one found by trial and error. What's new is its resurgence, particularly in the aftermath of well-publicized issues with mass-market drugs. But first, let us return to the start. Nearly every civilization utilized local flora to come up with their particular plant-based remedies. Thanks to every continent's diverse ecosystem, individuals in various countries relied upon unique remedies made out of their indigenous plants. Modern medications and remedies are inaccessible in several regions around the Earth; therefore, herbal healers continue to play a key public health function. Called the Edwin Smith Papyrus and Papyrus Ebbers following the guys who discovered them, these Egyptian historical functions incorporate extensive descriptions of notes on harms, and data on herbal pharmacology, together with designs for surgical and medical tools. Traditional African medicine focuses on herbal treatments, relying upon a pure drugstore with roughly 4,000 native plants.

Pharmaceutical companies recognize the value of Africa's herbal medications, studying from local professionals and utilizing conventional treatments to determine bioactive agents which may be employed to prepare contemporary synthetic medications. Ancient literature describing Chinese herbs' use was discovered in Changsha, China, in the Marandi Han tombs closed in 168 BCE. Traditional Asian medicine comprises massage, massage, acupuncture, and herbal remedies, together with dietary treatment. From the end of the sixteenth century, conventional Asian doctors had roughly 1,900 treatments at their disposal. From the end of this twentieth century, the Chinese

Materia medica comprised 12,800 distinct drugs. In India, a significant sourcebook known as the Atharva Veda laid down Ayurveda's fundamentals, a therapeutic practice that started around 1200 BCE. This system remains in use today. Ancient Middle Eastern doctors have discovered herbalists who taught Greek and Mexican scholars. Afterward, Arabs shared their understanding of European crusaders, who subsequently brought it back for their nations. Although Australia was visited by European boats in the 1600s, native and imperialist cultures collided in 1788 when Britain's First Fleet attracted about 1,500 individuals to Sydney. Since the last remaining practicing priests pass off, fewer rituals occur, and much more information about the continent's most medicinal flora is missing. Today, indigenous antipsychotic medication is known as bush medication. The clinic centers around conventional treatments using Australian seeds and leaves.

Native blossoms and banksia flowers can also be regarded as valuable regional remedies, while Chamomile and garlic are prized worldwide. Ancient Greek and Roman doctors were famous for their herbal knowledge. Much of that which they understood was passed down from Egyptian doctors. When the Roman Empire fell, technological advancement came to a stop, and much comprehension of herbal medication was missing. As trade with other cultures increased, however, understanding of medicinal herbs climbed again. Throughout the Renaissance, European nobles tried to curate all of the human knowledge from vast libraries; within their houses, they made remarkable efforts to build the beneficial botanicals of their moment. In 1652, Nicholas Culpeper printed The English Doctor, a thorough herbal catalogue of England's famous herbal remedies. The book was intended for ordinary folks, focusing on using herbs to cure common maladies rather than using expensive concoctions ready by physicians. Since the scientific era dawned, the prevalence of herbal treatments waned. Herbal remedies were almost forgotten with modern medications' arrival but are once more gaining popularity throughout Europe. Shamanic traditions continue today, employing exactly the identical plant medications which were revered for thousands of years. This continent is home to many plants with many medicinal applications, and traditional healers, or herbalists, could be found promoting their treatments in market stalls. The herbal knowledge, which still exists in remote jungle places, is immense.

Ancient Mayan and Aztec healers had used many different remedies made with therapeutic plants. They also claimed hospitals in which ill individuals were isolated by the remainder of their community while getting the attention and care they needed. However, South America provides an abundance of medicinal plants within its deep jungles. New species are found often, highlighting both the demand for conservation and also the prospect of promising treatments for ailments such as malaria and cancer. Today, over three-quarters of this world uses herbal medication. Western scientists have demonstrated in research that generations have passed down for centuries: Plants grown and utilized at home are good at treating non-life-threatening ailments, and injuries or disorders such as lumps, bruises, headaches, fever, anxiety, depression, tiredness, and much more. It is reasonable. You may toss them at a garden salad since they add shouts of taste, but those very same spices, herbs and, sometimes, vegetables, do double-duty once within the human body. They take antioxidants and nutrients which strengthen the immune system to resist disease before it begins. In contemporary physician's circles, they call that "preventative" medicine. Why wouldn't those very same herbs be used as efficiently for recovery after you have gotten sick? Chamomile makes a beautiful after-dinner tea, or you could use it to alleviate indigestion, relieve muscle cramps, reduce redness or heal infections.

1.2 Native American Herbal Medicine

Native American and First Nations people have been utilizing nature's medications for thousands of years, focusing on healing the body in addition to purifying the soul and balancing the brain. Cosmetic traditions passed down throughout the ages imply that the initial Mothers learned how to use medicinal herbs by detecting sick animals. As information was passed through word of mouth, there are no written records of native North Americans utilized herbs before their initial contact with Europeans. But this changed as native folks shared their natural treatments using the new settlers, a lot of whom brought with them knowledge of European herbal medicine. Many colonists introduced their favorite healing plants together into the New World. As time passed, herbal treatments had been mostly replaced with drugs like those used in Europe. For thousands of years, Native Americans have used herbs to cure the human body; however, they also purify the soul and balance their lives and environment.

- Oral traditions indicate they heard about herbs' healing powers and other crops by seeing sick animals. There are no written documents of herbal usage by the native people of America before this initial contact between Europeans and the tribes. But this changed as Native Americans shared their understanding of how to utilize nature's medicines using the settlers.

- While there have been hundreds of plants and herbs used in Native American remedies, among the very sacred was tobacco, that was utilized curing numerous conditions, in addition to ceremonies and rituals. It had been smoked pure and never mixed with any compounds because it has become today. One other essential herb into the Native Americans has been Sage, that was stated not just to cure several issues of the gut, kidneys, colon, liver, lungs, skin, and even much more, it was also thought to protect against bad spirits and to draw them from the human body or the spirit. Although the record of medicinal herbs which may be carried at a Healer's medication bundle are numerous and diverse, those who were most frequently used were often carried, for example, remedies for frequent colds which could comprise American Ginseng or Boneset; herbal supplements such as aches and pains such as Wild Black Cherry, Pennyroyal, and Hops; treatments for fever, such as Dogwood, Feverwort, and Willow Bark. This listing consists of many herbs used by Native Americans and others, which were proven to be beneficial for various ailments throughout history.

- Additionally, it includes herbs used for all of today's ailments. In reality, some folks still use these early herbal remedies today. Herbal remedies were an essential part of the Native American civilization that went much beyond treating the symptoms of disorders and to spirituality as part of this treatment.

Since different tribes developed treatments based upon what has been available to these, there are several distinct treatments for the same ailments. The allure of topics such as Native American herbal medicine is driven by the understanding that herbal remedies aren't as poisonous and with no side effects of several of today's prescription drugs. Some Native American treatments that were made utilizing North American plants are easy to track down and common to many locations, such as Skunk Cabbage. Wildcrafting is a contemporary clinic with historical origins, with lots of Wild crafters situated in North America. Wildcrafting is a worldwide clinic, together with individuals from various countries worldwide harvesting and using herbs, flowers, mosses, mushrooms and much more to practice natural recovery. It is the re-emergence of those manners of yesteryear. The Prevalence of Wildcrafting is pushed by the significance of historical treatments such as that used in Native American herbal medication and other ancient civilizations' medications.

1.3 When to Use Herbs

Each scenario requiring medical care differs, and every one of us as people responds differently to therapy. But here are a few tips for recognizing when herbal remedies can be a much better option than allopathic medical remedies: Preventative medication. They nourish the profound inner ecology of the systems on a cellular level. Herbs can also be powerful adaptogens, raising the body's capacity to adapt to the ever-changing surroundings and migraines of life, for many non-emergency medical scenarios. Herbs may also be a powerful "on the spot" first-aid remedy for emergencies where medical aid is unavailable or in its way. Suppose you decide to undergo more radical therapy types for serious illnesses like cancer, AIDS, multiple sclerosis, and other autoimmune diseases. In that case, herbs function as excellent secondary healing agents, encouraging and enhance your body's life.

Herbs and allopathic medication work compatible with such essential conditions and may be utilized to match and improve one another's effects. However, there, actually complementary and work together really compatibly. Whereas allopathic drugs knowingly kill germs and viruses, herbal medications restore and build the immune machine. Allopathic medication normally has a certain schedule; herbaceous plants, through an intricate biochemical process, take the entire person into account and rejuvenate your system at a cellular level. When taken properly, herbs don't upset the body's inherent sense of stability. Therefore, there are no or few side effects. Utilizing herbal remedies to match pharmaceuticals frequently will help remove or reduce the side effects of medication therapies.

- Though many of the most powerful herbs shouldn't be utilized together with allopathic drugs, many herbs don't interfere with pharmaceuticals' activities. They may be used to augment allopathic remedies. (Not one of these "powerful" herbaceous plants are called for this particular publication.) There's an increasing body of information regarding drug/herb interactions. However, it is essential to be aware that most of this study is in its baby stage. People today respond differently to herbal medicine and pharmaceutical medication. As a result of this, if you are thinking about using herbal medicine and taking a prescription, you need to talk to a holistic healthcare practitioner, who understands and knows herbal medication, to establish if herbs are advised on your circumstance. Herbs are among the safest drugs available in the world. There aren't poisonous plants or herbal remedies, resulting in unwanted effects or harmful reactions in the human body. The herbs that we use today are used for hundreds of years by individuals around the globe. Herbs with toxic side effects are noted and well recorded; sensibly, most of these herbs aren't available for sale within this nation. Sometimes an herb will provoke an idiosyncratic response in a person. It will not create the herb poisonous, only a bad selection for that specific individual. Strawberries, a flavorful fruit, are sweet buds to a noxious material to others. Wheat, another benign food, is an allergen into some high number of individuals and can result in dire consequences within a couple of.

There are lots of reports surfacing these days concerning the toxicity of herbaceous plants. Even entirely benign substances such as peppermint and Chamomile are finding themselves around the "blacklist" I. believe that the main reason behind this isn't that more people are using herbs, as is frequently suggested. S. Still, people are using herbs to allow more focused dosages. Still, herbal capsules that enable people to consume larger quantities and standardized pieces of training can be far past the standard concentrations found in nature haven't been available until recently. Any herb, the safest and most researched of herbaceous plants, can affect unique individuals differently. Even though it's a rare event, ginseng's negative frequently reported in the information makes national headlines, creating a particular alert among plant users. Were medication reactions reported with the same enthusiasm, we would have a nationwide headline aspirin each day. However, infrequent these responses to herbs may be that it's always Sensible to practice caution when utilizing an herb for the first time, mainly if administered to kids.

Chapter 2: Benefits & Uses of Herbal Medicine

Herbal medicine requires using crops to prevent or cure illness. We are aware that the oldest civilizations utilized plant-based remedies. Today, over three-quarters of this world uses herbal medication. Western scientists have demonstrated in studies that generations have passed down for centuries: Plants grown and utilized at home are good at treating non-life-threatening ailments, and injuries or disorders such as lumps, bruises, headaches, fever, anxiety, depression, tiredness, and much more. It is reasonable. Take all of the plants you consume regularly (yep, the very same ones that you pull out of the backyard or the produce section of your favorite grocer): parsley, cilantro, sage, Chamomile, garlic, ginger, ginger, mint. You may toss them at a garden salad since they add shouts of taste, but those very same spices, herbs and, sometimes, vegetables, do double-duty once within the human body. They take antioxidants and nutrients which strengthen the immune system to resist disease before it begins. In contemporary physician's circles, they call favorite. Why wouldn't those very same herbs be used as efficiently for recovery after you have gotten sick? St. John's Wort seems fantastic in a vase, but it's also excellent for reducing stress.

Chamomile makes a beautiful after-dinner tea, or you could use it to alleviate indigestion, relieve muscle spasms, decrease inflammation or heal infections.

- Herbal medicine is a favorite choice for treating health troubles or keeping a healthy way of life. These medications are composed of 100% organic ingredients in plants and creatures that may target certain regions in the body and encouraging their function. As a cost-effective remedy to common ailments and significant ailments, herbal medications are rather popular with ordinary individuals that can't afford costly modern medical remedies.

- Modern people of Asian nations, such as China and Japan, are proven to practice herbal medications in their everyday life since early times. Regardless of how herbal medicines use natural ingredients because of its makeup, this kind of therapy still has some dangers when it isn't correctly treated or administered to a person. In most instances, in using any type of drugs, malpractice, which entails inaccurate prescription and directions, can be fatal to your body. To prevent this issue, it's ideal for practicing caution regarding consulting a specialist and buying the medication you're choosing in this type of alternative treatment procedure. First, you have to refer to a physician, physician, or herbalist regarding which sort of herbal medication would best address your health issues.

- Throughout the consultation, they'll be asking you a definite question concerning the status of your well-being, in addition to the drugs that you're taking to take care of it. It's ideal to answer them honestly, considering their prescription and directions will solely rely on your response. Another element that includes the health dangers of herbal medications is the real product itself. If you're planning to buy the medication in raw type in almost any retail store in your region, then you better be sure there aren't any other herbs blended into it.

If you're planning to acquire commercialized herbal products in retail shops, then it's wise that you only buy from reputable and dependable businesses. You may want to speak with your physician if they could refer you to a broker or a shop that can offer you these excellent products to assist you in your treatment. However, the risk factor in picking the wrong solution, in addition to malpractice in both you and together with all the professionals that you consulted regarding this matter, is quite much clear. Page

In the ancient world, there were no health care physicians. If individuals become unwell, they'd visit the village older to understand the healing effects of different plant leaves, stem, flower and root, which grew wild in the regional all-natural environment. Medication from herbs is just one of the earliest forms of health care. It's a long and honored record of plants and

tonics goes back into our ancestors thousands of years previously. Each of the strategy back to 2800 B.C. Scientists and storytellers have reported humans experiencing the excellent therapeutic and healthiness advantages of herbal remedies. And now it's your opportunity!

In reality, the herbal remedy was a massive bit of human history for the past 5,000 years based on archaeology and in published documents. Each of the methods up to now, folks have utilized herbal remedies and remedies to encourage an expansive selection of diseases to better their healthiness and well-being. Many herbs have a very long history of use and nearly guaranteed healthiness advantages. An herb, or blossom, is a vegetal or part of an herbal (such as the stem just) which can be used for its odor, taste, or curative skills.

Even though they are located in ordinary, herbal products aren't guaranteed to be secure or brief of unwanted side effects. While they may come from crops, many plants (such as certain mushrooms) are harmful and may be hazardous or harmful to well-being, instead of preventing it. Unlike prescription medications, herbal products aren't clinically tested and demonstrated to work for a couple of specific ailments until they're marketed or sold to clients within healthiness nutriment stores such as GNC (General Nutrition Centers).

Additionally, the active ingredients at a great deal of herbal nutritional supplements and remedies wait unknown. Some supplements have been discovered that a few include compounds, prescription medications mixed in brief of a couple of mention on the label, microorganisms or a different substance. Because most herbal products aren't tested and accredited by way of the FDA or another well-being jurisdiction, they could, in real fact, source well-being issues or complications. All this is very uncommon because most companies accomplish their particular testing and just use the herbs' valuable kinds within their herbal products.

> Nonetheless, it couldn't be wise to try herbal products, at least afore talking about it together with your healthcare practitioner, even if you own medical problems if you're nursing or pregnant, at the moment you should take from the normal care about utilizing herbal products, by way of well by way of if you're about to possess operation. It is another pretext for its huge popularity of herbal remedies. To constantly be on the different facet of things, be sure you always consult your health care provider before attempting several herbal products you have concern yourself about.

> It's advisable to speak with your professional afore employing a herbal thing if you're taking a few medicines for a healthiness issue. Herbal nutritional supplement willpower often does not interfere with prescription medicine or over-the-counter medication, but it is always best to consult your healthcare practitioner.

➤ If you are just using herbs to increase your meals' flavor, you might be passing up a ton of untapped health advantages. Today, as more and more clinical trials demonstrate the effectiveness of particular herbs, what had formerly been disregarded, science is presently discovering a valid treatment option for numerous unique ailments. Ian Lloyd, a pharmacist and drugstore in Victoria, BC, states that 80 percent of his patients are currently using herbals, plus they are predominately girls. "As a pharmacist, I am always taking a look at the clinical signs, and there is an excellent sign that herbals will help for sure problems," he states. "Plus, my patients are continuously inquiring about herbals since they would like to care for their health." For people who are thinking about researching herbals, choices abound.

➤ You may need to experiment to discover what works best for you. Tinctures, by way of instance, are highly concentrated and much more readily digested than nutritional supplements but frequently have a sour alcohol base. Just like any new therapy, it is vital to allow your pharmacist, doctor and other health care providers to know any herbals you are thinking about if they interact with other drugs, " says Lloyd. By way of instance, herbs such as feverfew and ginseng should not be blended using warfarin and other blood thinners since the mix increases your chance of bleeding. If it comes to the roots of several ailments, including cancer, arthritis, depression and diabetes, chronic inflammation isn't ever a fantastic thing. But garlic, the principal spice found in curries from the garlic plant, proves to be quite an effective anti-fungal agent. A highly effective antioxidant that is more powerful than vitamins E and C, that this herb is famous for boosting the immune system and may be obtained each day on a long-term foundation.

If you're getting sufficient sleep and still feel lethargic, maca might be a capsule worth contemplating. Inspired by a plant that grows on the Andes mountains' greatest plateaus, it's been touted for improving endurance, energy, and libido. It's been traditionally utilized to balance female hormones, and clinical trials have demonstrated its efficacy in treating menopause symptoms. Huge amounts of data gathered from animal and human studies indicate that this herb, which can be located in North America and southern Asia, can considerably increase cognitive and physical capacity. Since ginseng is strong stuff, avoid taking it with stimulants (such as caffeine) and consult your physician to determine whether it is safe for you before attempting it. Earth issues are among the concerns that the majority of us incurred apart from fiscal matters.

The growth of different new dangers in people's well-being brings consciousness in various ways about the best way best to strengthen the immune system. Among the newest fads in being healthy would be choice medications that health-conscious men and women use. In the speed of intensifying health problems in order the herbal medications' popularity. Herbal medicines are natural, mostly from crops, but today it was commonly called nutritional supplements. The use of those herbal medications is dated back to early times. For the health-conscious individual that does not need the standard physicians prescribed medication, herbal medication is a great choice in treating simple illness to more significant ones such as cancer. Apart from less costly, herbal medications are famous for not having unwanted effects. Among the popular herbal medications, the majority of us beverage is tea. People today drink tea emperor in the first period without understanding the complete benefits of drinking it. Today, tea is highly considered an alternative medication for metabolism as well as other severe illness. Tea's advantages are a handful with this tiny leaf. Like its advantages, tea variations are many, and each is famous in treating some illness though all of the tea variations are good and beneficial for your health. When you consider the herbal remedies, then there are unique questions that roam on your thoughts.

Therefore, the occurrence of herbal remedies is challenging to gulp down too many. On the other hand, the background of herbal medications has demonstrated its effectiveness frequently. Regardless of the criticism among different areas of the planet, many individuals still adore Ayurveda's high effect in treating their varicose veins within the moment. There are numerous common medications derived from plant-based sources for curing the most frequent congenital ailments due to their broad benefits. In the origins of the tips, distinct components of a plant are utilized to reap the advantages. The allopathic drugs are created with most substances, which damage the human body and respond somehow. The artificial chemicals and plant and animal-based ingredients may worsen the issues. On the other hand, Ayurveda's healing ability has many advantages that barely possess any unwanted effects on the human body or mind. Natural plant compounds are used worldwide in treating several common and a few of the very complicated issues. They have many benefits to heal the issues efficiently and also have banished them by the roots.

There's nothing more empowering than simply taking control of your health. As a result of herbal medication's ability, together with your knowledge about the most effective ways to utilize it and the science of modern delivery methods, you are in a position to fully experience its advantages using secure, do-it-yourself methods on your own house. There is no guesswork about if they are harmful. They are not. (Hazardous herbs are not available commercially.) Should you encounter any impacts you did not expect from utilizing a herb, and then it is likely because of the total required --you have overindulged. Any discomfort is the brief term, the time it requires the chemicals to depart from your system. 1 guideline: If you are allergic to some plant, herb, or spice, then you are allergic to the essential oils, also.

They are cheap. Slimming down, homegrown herbs are less expensive than prescription meds, despite a copay! They are easily available. Even if you don't own a farm or garden, your windowsill gets the ideal platform for developing potted herbs you may play in the kitchen. Herbal plants are clinically tested to encourage the advantages claimed to comprise in each plant. These studies have been acknowledged and recognized by the medical community to demonstrate effectiveness in taking care of many disorders. Amala, by way of instance, is known to comprise elements for anti-diabetes. This claim to the effectiveness of amalaka as a help to deal with diabetes was clinically proven by several studies that have identified amalaka to feature plant insulin, which enriches the patient's blood glucose and inhibits insulin production within the body.

2.2 Uses of Herbal Medicine
It's remarkable knowledge that before the contemporary world of medicine came into being, individuals of the older world and a reasonable lifetime. Ever thought about how they did this? Through the Chinese culture's heritage, you may always encounter herbs. They used them because of their cooking and their own health care needs. These weeds and herbs held the religious connection, so they were used in prayers and other sacred rituals. The Native American Indian culture used

blossoms; they had a solid link with character, and they lived on it. Another distinction between contemporary age medicines and organic herbs is that they don't consist of heavy obligation titles. But herbs don't take unwanted effects as chemically improved medicines do. And they're not overly expensive.

Nowadays, people feel that if you pay very good money, you get the very best product; however, that's not accurate; quality matters. So, do you rather pay a fantastic deal for medications from the market than heading out to your backyard and plucking free and effective herbs to your therapy? When you consume, you use herbs for cooking functions; otherwise, you don't like the meals. It demonstrates they are great for health. The herb medicine method is called Home therapy. Conventional character physicians are those dealing with this.

Common herbal remedies incorporate using Chamomile to get flues. All you need to do is set a couple of Chamomile into a kettle of boiling water and inhale the vapor from beneath a blanket. It's a certain point manner of getting rid of this flu. Herbal remedies did come into being by accident, but since they've been polished and worked on. They consist of uses and benefits which were since studied and appeared deeply into. Even today, particularly today, science wars together with the organic world on the medication's power. But It's common sense to have religion in natural remedies instead of chemically enriched products that do possess unwanted effects.

Chapter 3: Making Herbal Medicine at Home

The quickest, simplest way to start is with a little garden, while it's in your yard or on a counter. Doing this joins you to the origin of your recovery and enables you to take as much care of your herbs since you do your brain, body, and soul. If you have already got a backyard, life just got easier. Medicinal herbs are a breeze to integrate into figurines or plots you have already obtained growing. Then you will have to spot the kinds of herbal preparations that draw you, anything from tinctures to teas and all in between. This publication can allow you to opt for the proper herbs on your own and the most effective strategies to prepare them for your needs and lifestyle. No worries if you are not a master chef or possess a love-hate relationship with your kitchen. Making herbal remedies does not require any particular skills or abilities, instead of real interest in your well-being and a small moment.

3.1 Basics of Herbal Preparation

After growing or buying the herbaceous plants that are appealing to you, you're going to be prepared to start making preparations. Each preparation has its purpose and targets specific topics and concerns, but isn't plant-specific, which means that you can mix and match your concoctions using various procedures. Each section intends to educate you regarding the herbal strategy and contain application procedures, the kitchen equipment you will want to create, and the storage containers you will want to have portions of the plant used for medicinal purposes depending on the monitoring and testing of native men and women. Usage of leaves, blossoms, stems, berries, and plants' roots to prevent, alleviate, cure, and treat different medical conditions is called herbal medicine.

Many contemporary drugs are derived from the understanding of herbs and their therapeutic properties. The medicinal part of the plant, plant, berry or root is dispersed and examined. This element is then artificially stabilized and fabricated in massive labs for use in pharmaceutical preparations. Before the discovery and synthesis of antibiotics, Echinacea was a widely researched medication to resist disease. It was part of this medical kit for those guys going to war. Today's scientists have discovered that their immune-boosting properties support the body to produce infection-fighting white blood cells. From the 1900s, as the Western medication developed, scientific study in the art to a science, modern medicine generated pharmaceutical labs based on artificial counterparts of medication made from herbs became increasingly popular, pushing the custom of ancient traditional herbal medication comparative obscurity. The World Health Organization has investigated that from 119 plant-based synthetic medication, 74 percent are prescribed identical therapeutic properties because native people have used it as an herbal medicine for centuries.

Pharmacologists identify, extract and isolate the active ingredient and synthesize it at the labs. The resultant strong medicinal grade of the energetic ingredient gets poisonous, creating unwanted effects. It will become poisonous since it's been removed from the normal surroundings. Another crucial supportive element of the plant, such as vitamins, minerals, bioflavonoids, volatile oils, glycosides, vitamins, alkaloids, etc., which improve their energetic element properties, have been removed. The herbal medication that has been initially secure has a synthetic counterpart, which has unwanted side effects. Herbal medications in their natural kinds are secure and don't typically suffer from unwanted effects and therefore are apt at fixing targeted issues. Herbs and herbal medicine can be found in several distinct types with exceptional properties for curing various medical ailments. They Can Be Found in the Shape of raw herbs, tinctures, capsules, extracts, pills, tablets, and additives.

2.1 Benefits of Herbal Medicine

Today, it's no surprise to comprehend that the whole thing tagged in place of herbal or regular. In only about a couple of shop, you go in, all you see are countless herbal or all-natural products in addition to dietary supplements and herbal medicine solutions. So, when did this herbal product happening begin? One retort is that it started when the media started to report commonly on precisely how vital it's to keep up a wholesome diet and lifestyle. Understanding the advantages of herbal medications and routine available. Preceding the part on cosmetic care training is a Know Your Skin Care guide that will help you figure out which treatments will work well with your skin type. It isn't anything mysterious or even especially clever or skillful in making recovery formulas from crops. Not so! If it's possible to produce a cup of tea or cook a simple meal, your loved one's members and friends are prepared to eat, and you're qualified.

Numerous methods of using plants to discharge and trigger their therapeutic properties have grown over time. Without a doubt, our remote ancestors used herbs simply by eating the new plant. Since that time, many different techniques of preparation have already been developed. Together with our contemporary understanding of pharmacology, we could make conscious decisions about which procedure we use to discharge the biochemical components required for recovery without diluting this plant's integrity by isolating fractions of the entire world. Several excellent herb publications now available include comprehensive manuals to making herbal preparations. The best method of using herbs would be to take them from within that recovery. The manners of preparing internal treatments are many, but in most cases, it's crucial to take good care of the procedure to guarantee the desired outcome. Three types of pieces of training are used for internal ingestion: eucalyptus extracts (teas), tinctures, and dried or fresh herbs in capsule or pill form. Recipes for herbal preparations are extremely simple to create at home. Some have only a few steps where others have many measures, but they're all relatively simple. Discover how to create a herbal infused oil. Or try your hand at blending teas using this specific digestive aid herbal tea or even an adaptogen chai tea mix!

The thought of creating your topical medications and formulas from organic ingredients might appear somewhat daunting, but it shouldn't be. It is simple and soul-satisfying and maybe a great deal of fun. Just basic kitchen gear and cooking abilities are essential for creating superbly new, health-and wellness-nurturing creations. It is an easy and ancient art that everyone can do. "Cleanliness is next to godliness" -- there is a fantastic reason I state this in virtually every organic body-care publication I write. Ideally, all implements ought to be boiled, but that is not necessarily practical or even possible. Give them a great wash, wash them and wash them well. The objective is to minimize the potential for damaging bacterial growth on your preservative-free goods.

3.2 Buying and Storing Herbs

It's very important to insist on high quality, ideally organically grown herbs. Though these herbs can cost a few cents more, they're far better to our medications and, finally, our world. Have available in any way times a minimum of two ounces of those herbs you intend on using. And do not use herbs from the country or elsewhere, which are endangered or at risk from the wild. It ought to seem, taste and odor almost just as it will when new, and it ought to be effective. Dried herbs should possess a vibrant color. Although they might not necessarily odor "great," they ought to odor powerful. Again, they might not taste "great"; gauge their flavor by effectiveness instead of taste. Should you discover one of your herbal remedies isn't successful, look at the herbs' grade you utilized to create it. I've traveled extensively, and I am astounded by the gaps in herbs' standard in various areas of the earth. From the first days of herbalism in the USA, our herbaceous plants' standard was quite poor. Still, within the past three decades, there's been this emphasis on utilizing high-quality herbs in which people now lead the world in quality criteria. We're expecting to get the same impact globally about the preservation of medicinal plant inhabitants. If we want to preserve this healing method for our kids, protecting medicinal plant species becomes more critical. You're encouraging not just your health but also the health of the world when you buy organic and sustainably harvested herbs.

Herbs keep their possessions best if kept in airtight glass jars, away from direct light, at a trendy location. For convenience, you can save them in several different containers -- containers, tins, plastic bags -- but many meticulous herbalists find lasting glass bottles that the very best for storage. Each herb has its shelf life, and observing a set rule may indicate that you would throw out fine peppermint while utilizing poor-quality chickweed. As previously explained, you may quickly ascertain whether a specific herb has kept its characteristic: Does it smell powerful?

Is its colour vivid? Does this taste refreshing? If so, regardless of what the books say about shelf life, It's probably still good.

3.3 Shopping for Herbs

High-quality herbs are high-quality herbs, irrespective of their source. Where you live, that may be a local health food shop, a tiny community farm, or perhaps your neighbor's backyard. You might even have a herb store locally. Cheaper isn't usually better! Local tiny manufacturers frequently have to charge more because of their herbal and herbal products; however, the grade is also often greater. Experiment with little batches initially, which means you learn which manufacturers have the very best quality, allowing you to understand whether it is well worth the cost.

There are several things to bear in mind while sourcing herbaceous plants: soil quality, growing practices, and how they are processed or dried. If the soil in which the herbs have become contaminated with heavy metals or other contamination, this is likely to be from the plant issue. You must understand where the herbaceous plants have been grown, which means that you can learn whether the soil has been sterile. It is sometimes troublesome for herbs grown everywhere, particularly those grown in areas that don't have regulations regarding land contamination. For example, some bigger herb retailers, Mountain Rose Herbs, examine their herbaceous plants to be certain that they're free from soil-based contamination.

You may be disinclined to buy herbs developed in urban farms, but do not write them off: Speak to the manufacturers and inquire in their land. Most urban farms bring in fresh soil and utilize water filtration to ensure that their manufacture is secure. How were insects handled? What type of fertilizer has been used? Were the herbaceous plants grown in a greenhouse or outside? These items have pros and cons, but the main point is that the result: In the event the blossoms have vibrant colors and powerful aromas and tastes, then the grade is great. The processing and drying step can be complicated, too: lean blossoms may be destroyed if they are dried at too high a temperature or stored improperly. You will understand that this is true if there's significant browning from the dried herbs. It is precisely the identical browning you'd see on a living plant with brown, dried foliage --it seems un-vital. For instance, let us use St. John's wort: This plant must have brownish when it is dried, but its brownish shade is deep-red mahogany. That is different from the brown-black color of basil leaves, which have gone bad on your fridge. The most important thing is, know that you are buying your herbs out of. Does this help you make good choices, but it can also help build community between the men and women who develop our herbs (and meals) and those who eat them. When we herb (and meals) and those people who swallow the.

3.4 Growing Herbs

The prerequisites for suitable growth of herbs differ from acidic soil needs to fit soil requirements. The publication that will follow will cover each one of these variables on an herb by plant foundation. It can be worth remembering that if I had been educated herbal medicine, both the Chinese and Native American, I had been taught a very simple method that generally ensured achievement. Though there's little understood by most of those similarities of those techniques, I'll outline them here. Several civilizations several hundred years back were traveled, from great hunting and collecting areas to other places when match and consumable forage was no more abundant. These tribes would collect the herbs as they discovered them and dry them to make tinctures for future usage. Other tribes that were geographically stable, like the Cherokee that built log houses and the Pueblo that constructed their houses in mountainsides, cultivated the most often used herbs.

The method was straightforward, and many growths were performed through transplantation and development in seeds. In transplantation, plants had been shot with a massive dirtball stored at the bottom of this plant. Symbols that reflected that the terrain they were obtained from and the way they confronted were noted. The chunks of soil were subsequently utilized to match dirt around the tribal territory as closely as you can. Often the dirt was tasted to ascertain its acidity or alkalinity along with other aspects. When planting from seeds, the same procedure was used, just dirt from the plant the seeds gathered from was obtained for a game. These techniques were nearly always used on quite rapidly growing plants. Some plants used in medication were obtained from mature trees or quite slow growth herbs, for example, American Ginseng, and those were only gathered when discovered. American Ginseng became so precious that uncontrolled herbal crafters nearly wiped it out from the USA. The folks taking even immature crops available should be depended on, and the item shouldn't be found from them.

They've nearly eliminated among the most versatile herbs within our nation. While seeing Bucharest, I had been taken to one of the biggest herbal providers in the entire world that routinely provided high-quality herbal products of wonderful diversity. Its goods were tidy and reliable since they were tracked from planting to harvesting. This firm was responsible for providing all the Soviet Union before its split but was attempting to find markets to substitute the prior demand. The purpose is lots of herbs will require far too much time to develop to help your consumption. Some others develop at altitudes and at other extreme conditions, which would be rather hard to replicate. The ones that develop around your area that you're readily able to develop, the previous approaches work well but might restrict your urge to produce the recipes you need. Because of such issues, I'd make the following proposal. If you discover a recipe on the internet or in our next publication and feel it will be useful, purchase them by a trusted source in their bulk form and operate with those you're unable to develop yourself. I'd recommend you create your tinctures out of the entire herb you've purchased from your trusted source. I do so because I understand the care, they take in obtaining sources and understand they simply sell herbs, which were grown cleanly and correctly with no additional pesticides. There are various shops such as this around, along with the great ones not mind being asked exactly what the resources for certain herbs are. The main reason I'm suggesting you make your tinctures out of the entire herb is a result of how a few businesses are proven to get rid of main actives from an herb, subsequently sold tinctures of the herb along with the actives individually to some other corporation. Simply because it says organic or has been an herbal item doesn't indicate it's either increased correctly or is complete in its active components.

The herbs that I use are constantly triple analyzed, not just for pollution, but also for percent of active chemicals to measure how much must be utilized to achieve the target. It is a costly and time-consuming procedure that you can't be expected to perform in your property. For your house herbalist, tinctures created from a trusted supply of the entire herb would be the safest and surest way to guarantee a trusted outcome. He wasn't expected to reside past a year. He was so feeble he was not able to get up off the ground when he got down. Besides radical dietary adjustments, and a fantastic multiple vitamin and vitamin nutritional supplement, I proposed a few other nutritional supplements, such as a cayenne tincture be obtained frequently. When requested, " I suggested that he use a well-known and decent selling merchandise he could purchase. I tried hard not to sell goods out of my workplace.

After a few months on such nutritional supplements and dietary modifications, he requested concerning the saltwater tincture. He said he'd read it and believed that he could make a much better tincture with the older method explained in this publication. At a little over eight weeks, he presented me with his homemade tincture to test. He explained it'd just taken five weeks to increase to pep species er he'd picked through his study and another three weeks to ready the tincture as is introduced in this publication. Darned if it was not 100% greater than that which he was buying. He'd researched the subject and made the proper decision in freshwater species and created the tincture that the way that they need to be made. From there on, I inquired if he'd mind making more of his tincture so that my additional sufferers that required it would use his. He had been pleased to perform this, and he never billed a single individual because of his product. Even with just a little research and excellent advice, you may earn a superior product should you choose the easy moral. Simply choose your sources carefully and rely upon the Easy directions and rely on our ancestors' knowledge, who have tens of thousands of years of expertise behind them. Herbs have several health benefits, from boosting your resistance to reducing cholesterol and blood pressure. The easiest way to utilize more herbs would be to develop your herb garden. If you grow herbs for your health, you can observe an improvement in physical and psychological well-being. Through the ages, people have discovered herbs to gain the mind, soul and body. It is amazing to find out about the benefits of herbal supplements.

Why don't you make the most of developing herbs for your health? If you frequently use herbs in cooking or about fries and might love to have simple access in your home to an abundant source of fresh herbs, then why don't you try growing your favorite herbs from seed in your garden? Though you might be only an herb gardening newcomer, it should not take quite a while until you take pleasure in the satisfaction of getting freshly-picked herbs to use in your recipes. If you decide to start developing your herbs from seed this year, the more seeds you sow in the spring could create abundant supplies of summer blossoms that could be utilized immediately. When you take a last crop of herbs at the close of the summer, this crop can be kept away to be used within the winter. You most likely already have thoughts about herbs you want to grow. When I was only beginning to grow herbaceous plants, I climbed basil from seed several years back since I needed fresh ginger to use my cooking. I know other herb gardening newbies began with herbs such as parsley, chives, and lavender since they used them to get their favorite recipes. But do not only use the herbs which are extremely comfortable for you. Take some research to generate a listing which contains these and a few less comfortable herbs. Additionally, take a look at the gardens of different people you understand that develop herbs, visit the regional garden center, and find out what herbs they're offering. Now the hard work is finished, you'll have the ability to begin harvesting your herbs in the first summer. Whenever you do this, do not remove too many leaves at the same time. You need every plant to keep on growing after harvesting.

Supplying you follow this straightforward harvesting rule, it's possible to harvest the herb over and over through the summer and into early autumn. You'll also have something to boast about in your next dinner party when you're complimented on the taste of the food you've prepared using your very own home-grown herbs! You will find many practical advice and suggestions about the best way to develop all kinds of sorts of unique herbs at home, both inside and outside. And as soon as you've grown your herbs, then learn about all the various methods of using these to help you produce great food and encourage a healthful way of life. The site is excellent for both beginners with no prior experience of herb growing and people who have experience but need to undertake a few more ambitious plants growing endeavors.

3.5 Harvesting of Herbs

It is a topic that may only be granted justice in a publication of its own. With this publication's goal, I'll provide the next chapter as a good example and give a couple of exceptions to start the learning procedure. It may also help you become knowledgeable about the most often used approaches and their benefits.

Harvesting of herbaceous plants is virtually always done while the herb is in its peak of ripeness or development. It's also the period that should be dried, and then they'll retain the maximum concentration of actives. If the fruit is your target, harvesting will occur once the fruit has attained adulthood. If the seeds would be the harvesting aim, you have to wait until the plant has grown, and the seeds are ready to be chosen in the plant.

The most significant thing to bear in mind is that the perfect time for harvesting plant components is to perform it if the plant includes the maximum quantity of desirable phytochemicals. Now I believe it's imperative to discuss how herbs have been quantified when utilizing complicated formulations or simple combinations. Because recipes were frequently traded between medication men and Orientals that could speak various dialects or utilize unique dimensions, a straightforward means to get around that problem was easily solved.

Dimensions were simply put into parts. A part was blended with 1or 6 or 3 components with the same measurement irrespective of the size or dimension. It may be a few particular cup size or easy jar dimensions, but the details were kept constant. Later in this publication, a couple of recipes have been given. The details are 1-1-1 on most tinctures used in those recipes. More complicated recipes will be in a coming publication; however, the dimension process will always be the same, and all recipes have been given this way. The most flexible system of communicating herbs is in building a tincture. Tinctures ordinarily have a secure shelf life of seven years, and could be added to animal or vegetable fats such as a wound or transdermal program, taken sub-lingual, orally, additional to teas, or put directly to wounds, used as a suppository if chilled or inside a poultice if needed. Each one of these activities relies on the functions for which the herbaceous plants were selected. Many plant compounds that can dissolve in alcohol won't be different in the water. The reverse is also correct. Many plant compounds which are soluble in water aren't soluble in alcohol. By utilizing a 50/50 mix of alcohol and water, we can get the maximum actives out of our herbs. There are always a few exceptions, but allow me to introduce the Native American way of creating the fundamental tincture. It is the old school process, but I have found it to be entirely trustworthy. If you're using whole herbs, then crush them before creating the tincture. Fill out a glass jar or other glass jar with an airtight lid using unpacked herbs you'll be using to create the tincture. It isn't important to use dried or fresh herbs; the technique is the same. When you've filled the jar using all the loose herbs, then pay for them with 100 cheap proof vodkas (100 proof includes a 50/50 mix of water and vapor). Shake the mixture well and set in a dark cabinet. Shake the mixture twice per day for 30 days. It's crucial to attempt and guard the tinctures against the sun as far as you can. When creating tinctures, consistently use glass containers, not utilize any aluminum. It can ruin the tincture and produce your difficult work useless. In innovative mixtures where reduced heat might be used, they need to contact nothing stainless steel. Aluminum is to be avoided. Becoming "old school" and after restructuring the outcomes of the other procedures, I firmly feel that the elderly method is ideal for extracting the maximum actives, even though it's more time-consuming. Lobelia should utilize just ethanol in extraction if it's going to be used internally. A number of these water-soluble actives may be somewhat toxic and shouldn't be used frequently.

The more surface area of the herbs vulnerable to this pulling substance, the more energetic the tincture will include. Shaking the bottles twice each day will ensure the spices are continuously agitated and will help in a more concentrated tincture. Suppose alcohol isn't desirable in what's to be utilized. In that case, the alcohol can readily be evaporated from the tincture by merely adding hot water for producing tea or simply by utilizing low heat. Too much heat can ruin the tincture, thus keep it under a simmer. You just have to get it hot enough to evaporate the alcohol. Alcohol will vanish much sooner compared to water. They should usually be utilized as new as you can. Many herbalists and homeopaths invest the spring-summer and fall in choosing their uncooked herbs and making their preparations in the late autumn and winter. It might be desired to maintain some herbaceous plant ground into powder form. These powders might be used to stop bleeding in wounds within their powder types and act as an antibacterial. These can need the tinctures to be blended with either hemp or olive oil or rendered fat from animal sources.

precisely the same next time, or create Sure you have the appropriate potency for the tincture.

3.7 Infusion from Plant

An extract is a tea made by pouring boiling water over fragile areas of the plant--such as leaves, fruits, dried flowers, berries, or buds--then steeping the liquid so that the nutrients have been imparted the beverage. Alternatively, you'll softly allow the steeping tea "free float" in a jar to make the most of extraction. This procedure permits you to get both the tastes as well as the nutrients in the herbs. You may use olive oil, in addition to new ones. Just make sure the dried herbs have not passed their shelf life, which reduces their healing power and effectiveness. When the herbs are strained off, your extract is about to drink. French media is a useful way to produce infusion.

3.8 Liniments & Tinctures

Tinctures are made by soaking herbs in a solvent--essentially, a chemical that dissolves other substances to produce a remedy. Alcohols like vodka and gin are the most common solvents used in tinctures, although apple cider vinegar is just another alternative increasing in popularity. The solvent operates by extracting the crucial substances in the herb. The mixture is then strained and moved into a dark bottle. Alcohols used in tinctures must maintain the 80-to 100-proof range for optimum extraction of herbal nutrients, essential oils, and other curative plant juices. Eighty to 90-proof alcohols also work if you are utilizing no juicy or dried herbs on your tincture. Most herbalists believe that when the concentration is made with anything. Aside from alcohol, it is not a tincture instead of an infusion.

3.9 Decoction Boiling Herbs

Delicate components of crops, decoctions are high profile herbal teas produced in the heartiest sections of crops, such as fibrous stalks, thick bark, seeds, nuts, or roots. As these elements tend to be on the more demanding, denser side, it requires a slow warmth to extract their minerals and healing components. To put it differently, only steeping them in boiling water is insufficient to discharge the powerful nutrients and the more decadent tastes inside these heartier, rougher combinations. (Prevent aluminum since it may cause a chemical reaction with a few herbs.) There is no set time limit on how long to boil or simmer. Instead, wait till the water decreases from two-thirds of its initial level, leaving an incredibly concentrated medicinal beverage. Strain off the herb mix before you drink the rest of the decoction.

3.10 Herbal Baths

Baths are similar to herbal teas to your body. Based on the types of herbs you use and the warmth of your water, your Prep can excite your senses or unwind them. By Way of Example, herbs like Rosemary or eucalyptus are ideal for night comfort, while peppermint and green tea make for excellent morning pick-me-ups. Herbal baths can create Fantastic healing success. Anxiety, stave off colds and influenza, alleviate inflammation, improve the mood, tone the Skin, also promote cell repair. Fundamentally, herbal baths are restricted only by Their particular therapeutic healing abilities. You may be amazed to understand how Beneficial bathing maybe with the herbs you have stashed in your refrigerator's crisper.

3.11 Herbal Balms and Slaves

Salves and balms are ointments developed to heal, shield, or soothe skin. From here, select your ingredients depending on the issues you are attempting to treat, like eczema, eczema, dry skin, chapped lips, bug bites, allergies, bloating, and much more. The majority of the herbs you will want are readily found in your garden or your windowsill and are teeming with skin-fixing nutrients and essential oils. Or, skip a step and begin with infused oils to have less doctoring up to perform. Both training pieces may vary in depth and ratio of oils to wax according to your taste and program requirements. But, they ought to comprise zero glasses of water or carbohydrates, both of which can be earmarked for preparing lotions and creams. Salves and balms are all intended to be placed topically on the skin for a vehicle for imparting recovery elements to your entire body.

3.12 Herbal Oils

You have essentially created an herbal oil if you have made salad dressing or chili oil for bread dipping. The one difference with the procedure described here's you will heat the oil and utilize herbs to target particular health problems. While there is a recent explosion of herbal nutritional supplements from the marketplace--including rosemary for scalp and hair, and calendula for skin disorders --they are not a new item. In reality, they have been employed for centuries to inject plants' healing nutrients to the epidermis. The types you will use in this publication are not any different from those you'll discover in a luxury spa therapy area or on department store shelves, but the purchase price tag is a lot lower. Olive oil is your go-to oil to get herbal medication since it is chock full of healthful fatty acids. Since it's a faint olive odor, you might not enjoy it for bath oils. However, it's the trick concerning moisturizing and nourishing your skin.

3.13 Herbal Teas

Herbal tea is a small misnomer since it is not technically a tea. By definition, tea is a beverage made by steeping the treated leaves of the particular tea plant (Camellia sinensis) in warm water and includes varieties like oolong, black, white, white, yellow, green. On the other hand, herbal tea is a mix of spices, herbs, and virtually anything else you would get from a plant indulged in hot or warm water. You can use bark, roots, blossoms, additives, fruit, balls of ginger or lemon --add to your list. Red tea, aka rooibos, also falls to the herbal class despite its title. One way to consider its that herbal teas are created from most anything you would see in the backyard is mint, chamomile, and echinacea. Even though most of the planet is quite sure about ingesting just the "authentic" teas, the United States is obsessed with herbal teas (thanks to their antioxidant levels, medicinal applications, and too little caffeine). It does not appear to obey the misnomer. Bearing this in mind, this publication employs the expression, tea, generically. As Soon as You understand the distinction between herbal and non-herbal teas, the very following thing to understand is there are two kinds of herbal teas: infusions and decoction.

3.14 You Must-Have Herbs

Concerning the herbs, you will need in your arsenal since they are exceptionally versatile super healers. Stock up on those fab five, and you will immediately have access to a source of recovery options in a vast assortment of training. Better yet, you may use them until you need them since the powerhouses in this chapter operate and prevent ailments because they do in curing them.

> **CHAMOMILE (German and Roman)**

In ancient times, chamomile has been called the "plant doctor" because where it had been planted, flowers and herbs round it had been treated and rejuvenated. In medical circles, chamomile has been researched and utilized worldwide to get a vast array of conditions, each unusually distinct. For example, it has been used to cure wounds, relieve PMS, cure Crohn's disease, reduce labor pains, and the list continues. Keep this "plant doctor" into your house, so it is available when you want a healing remedy. Twenty-six countries cannot be wrong. Chamomile has been accepted by over two dozen states to deal with chronic and severe issues and disorders, which range from inflammation and disease to colic, muscular strain, and pain. Its active ingredients include azulene, an antifever, anti-inflammatory substance, tannins, flavonoids, magnesium, calcium, magnesium, salicylates, and sour glycosides.

> **GARLIC**

Not sure why, but it's said that ancient Greek and Roman brides carried bouquets of garlic and other herbs, rather than gorgeous flower mixes, during their marriage ceremonies. Ancient Egyptians prized garlic, too. They fed it to the slaves who built the Great Pyramid, thinking it gave them super strength. Check out this listing of good-for-you This cocktail of nourishment boasts a remarkable success rate at battling heart disease, cancers, and disease, while boosting immunity, warding off colds, and draining the blood of toxins. That is well worth a bit of awesome breath.

> **PEPPERMINT**

Ancient Romans were on this herb Before modern medication. They nibbled on peppermint to improve their smarts, smelled the spice to maintain tempers quelled, and royals even put it into their own pockets for on-the-go recovery and energizing. It turns out; the Romans were late to the match. It is pleasant, refreshing, rejuvenating, and stimulating. Experts say it promotes memory, cognition, and endurance.

Contrary to a midday coffee shot, peppermint is revitalizing so that you do not possess the post-sip crash. What is its secret? The herb is chock full of flavonoids, phenolic acid, triterpenes, magnesium, calcium, magnesium, menthol, and menthone.

> **CALENDULA**

Calendula can Increase Your A game at the dinner table. Omelets, and more with a gourmet mindset, as a result of their brilliant Yellow-orange color. Their magnificent blooms mask among the best attributes: their heartiness. These flowers can defy premature snow and frost, while For DIYers, this implies calendula Does not want your green thumb. It may look after itself! Because of some Powerhouse roundup of ingredients such as bitters, volatile oils, Fixer for almost all difficulties from dehydration to severe issues. Its Nontoxicity makes it perfect for treating infants also, which makes it a go-to Diaper rash lotion. The herb can also be appreciated for its efficacy as an If that is not Sufficient, try it like an aromatherapy tool to keep skin young, luminous and Perfect.

> **ECHINACEA**

Native Americans seemed to echinacea as Their one-stop-shop for recovery. Early European explorers to the New World immediately caught on to the herb's magical and started using it to combat infections. At one stage in the nineteenth century, echinacea has been regarded as a "treatment for many more diseases than any other plant." More than only a cold fighter, this supplement boasts a lot of unique ingredients and nutrients such as caffeic acid, beta-carotene vitamin C, vitamin C, ellagic acid, polysaccharides, echinacoside, tannins, and sesquiterpenes. Request an herbalist, and they will probably tell you that this is the one most crucial immunity booster that you can have on your plant arsenal.

Chapter 4: Native American Herbs

4.1 Goldenseal Orangeroot

A native to North America, goldenseal was commonly used by Native American tribes to protect against nearly everything. Its primary active ingredients--berberine and beta-hydrastine--have massive anti-inflammatory and astringent benefits, not to mention it is a powerful antibacterial, antifungal, and decongestant. Typically seen in the wild, the vast market demand on this miracle herb has put its supplies at risk so beware of any goldenseal merchandise labels that don't say "organically cultivated" Perhaps you've heard through the grapevine about one of the goldenseal's most popular applications --to produce a false negative when urine is tested for prohibited drugs, from marijuana to cocaine. However, there is no hard evidence showing the goldenseal works for this purpose in line with the University of Maryland Medical Center.

or bladder issues. They are full of calcium, iron, and other trace minerals and value the world over delicious wild greens. The flowers make a glass of delicious wine. Dandelion root is decocted and served as a tonic tea for the liver. If tender, the root may be chopped just like a carrot and inserted into some soup or toaster. Dandelion has a sour zest to it; therefore, it is best when blended with milder herbs. My favorite way to eat the leaves would be to steam them and marinate them overnight in Italian dressing and honey.

4.5 Cayenne Herb

In case you cannot tolerate the heat, you may want to up your tolerance. Cayenne is much more than only a spicy blossom; it is a wellness superfood. This wonderful little spice does on your body exactly what it does to your mouth, makes things sexy quickly. It speeds recovery, quickens flow, ups metabolism, boosts immunity, and hair development. It is just like a shot of adrenaline directly to your wellness. Capsaicin, which dials up the pepper's warmth, was extensively studied because of its curative properties. Researchers have looked at over 300 research of its effects on metabolism and revealed that it does accelerate weight loss and mood desire. It is a hot herb and must be managed with caution, particularly for anyone who has sensitive skin. Wear gloves or wash hands thoroughly after use to prevent getting it into your eyes. Also, remember that big doses may upset your stomach. Less is more with saltwater.

4.6 Clove Aromatic

Clove is an incredibly nutrient-dense spice whose active ingredient, eugenol, was studied broadly. Filled with manganese, magnesium, iron, magnesium, vitamin K, and fiber, this miracle flower bud is admired for the anti-inflammatory, antiviral, antibacterial, and antimicrobial properties. Although studies have been inconclusive, it is used to supplement contemporary cancer treatment and remedies and other ailments such as hepatitis with positive outcomes. Since the eighth century, cloves were a significant part of the Asian and European trade. In reality, wars are fought within the spice. Clove is deemed safe when taken in quantities typically found in foods, but no studies are done taking the herb for medicinal use in the long run. The active ingredient in clove, eugenol, slows blood flow, so avoid eating clove post-surgery or when you are taking blood thinners. Cloves are the flowering buds of recurrent clove trees. They grow readily in moist, tropical locations or rich, reddish soil. Their perfect requirements are tight shade and rain.

4.7 Valerian Herb

It is most often considered "brain foods" since its sweet spot helps cure and encourage the nervous system. The first European colonists sent valerian together with all their possessions to begin a new life in the use. Since this herb is a natural strain and pain reliever that is simple to grow, packaging it because a cure-all has been a no-brainer is among my preferred nerve tonics and muscle relaxants. It functions well for many people; a small proportion of individuals find it annoying and too stimulating. It's useful for insomnia, pain, irritability, headaches, digestive issues because of nerves and muscle aches in people for whom it works. Based upon the person, the odor is relished or deemed offensive. I rather adore the smell, that reminds me of violets, or wealthy, sweet ground. Others might discover that Since the origin is full of volatile oils, it needs to be infused instead of decocted. Valerian is often tinctured or vaporized instead of taken as tea due to its odor, even though its flavor is very agreeable. Herbalists are in a debate about whether the dried or fresh herb functions better. I find it is an issue of personal taste. Indeed, it is better smelling and tasting when new, but I discover that the dried root functions in addition to the fresh root. Cats adore valerian root, too, more than catnip. Sprinkle some in their bed or on the ground for a few playful antics.

4.8 Comfrey Symphytum

This herb was an essential beauty ingredient with historical civilizations because of its skin healing, anti-aging, and youth-promoting consequences. It moisturizes, causes skin cell turnover, brightens, protects against germs, inflammation, redness, and soothes skin layers. It had been famous for healing broken bones from the Middle Ages, even though contemporary scientists have yet to affirm this specific remedy functions. It is not advised to take comfrey by mouth because of its pyrrolizidine alkaloids, leading to lung disease, cancer, and liver damage. You will love comfrey in your backyard since its vibrant blue and purple blossoms appear fantastic, it's easy to develop, and it contrasts beneath the shade of other plants and trees. The only downside is that if you want to get rid of it, then fantastic luck. Its origins are delicate, breakable, and sprout new plants quickly and efficiently.

4.9 Genus Aloe Vera

Apart from being simple to watch over, it is helpful to have available for on-demand first aid for burns, sunburns, scrapes, or any other skin condition. As it is packed with tannins, vitamins B and E, fiber, selenium, polysaccharides, silicon, and aloin, you are just as likely to find it within an over-the-counter ointment since you're on the menu using a juice bar. For more severe problems, such as arthritis pain, gut difficulties, or inflammatory conditions, many herbalists maintain a jar of aloe vera skin healing juice in their refrigerator to spike their morning cup of tea. Aloe is the most excellent beautifier, regarded as a critical weapon in Cleopatra's skincare regimen. Split open a leaf and apply the gel directly up as a cosmetics remover, hairdryer, or cuticle softener. There are brains behind its beautifying power, also. Studies have shown it could be effectively utilized to deal with asthma and diabetes.

4.10 Ginger

As an all-purpose cure-all and immunity booster (thanks to therapeutic ketones such as gingerol), ginger competitions its own culinary counterpart, garlic, in efficacy in treating many different conditions. You have probably already been appreciating its medicinal advantages if you are a lover of Thai, Indian, or Chinese cooking. Like garlic, you can get tremendous healing benefits by integrating the herb into your culinary regularly more frequently. From the thirteenth and fourteenth centuries, it is considered that a pound of ginger could put you back the purchase price of a single sheep. Despite its well-documented usage, nobody is sure of their plant's roots.

4.11 Ginseng Genus Panax

While ginseng has been a significant part of Traditional Chinese Medicine for thousands of years, it has only lately come into vogue in the USA, having been analyzed for an assortment of ailments and conditions which range from moderate to severe. The herb is a significant force in strengthening immunity and healing digestive, heart, and nervous system difficulties and healthy addition to an anti-aging beauty regimen. The English word ginseng derives from the term that means "individual" and "plant origin." The root's attribute forked shape looks like the legs of someone.

4.12 Hops Flowers

Hops are the female blossom of the plant that is mythical. If you have ever done a bar crawl, you are conscious of a few of the most significant medicinal advantages of hops: its stimulant effects. The herb has been demonstrated to be good at triggering weight reduction, treating menstrual disorders, calming anxiety, and balancing moods through the years. And not only when it is brewed and packaged using a beer can. It is used today in many different preparations, from teas to anti-aging skincare. As a result of its prevalence in home brewing (versus residence recovery), it is projected that almost three-quarters of jumps manufacturing were DIY at-home combinations in pre-war instances. (There is no record of how much has been drunk from a mug versus a place to a medication tincture.) Hops are deemed nontoxic and safe. But some individuals should take caution when using since they could make depression worse. They also stimulate estrogen, thus avoid if you have been diagnosed with breast cancer. Hops can also interact with anesthesia, causing the individual to undergo heightened consequences. Hops are proven to be harmful to puppies.

4.13 Hyssopus Officinalis

Hyssop gets its star power in the herbal Medicine world by its properties as an antiseptic, cough reliever, expectorant, and because of its aromatic qualities. Gourmet chefs revere it for the flavor-enhancing kick it gives to soups, stews, salads, and sauces. This herb was just another favorite of the Greeks, namely Hippocrates, Galen, and Discords. In their times, the herb was readily suggested for an assortment of issues--many popularly as a decongestant, disinfectant, and stimulant. Today, its anti-inflammatory benefits are sought by those who have muscle tension, neck pain, anxiety, or throat problems due to overworking their voices. Actors, public speakers, singers, politicians, teachers, and many others may find hyssop's performance quite useful. Add its essential oils into a carrier oil. It creates a fantastic massage or bath oil or combines with just about any oil to get a nourishing, antibacterial facial treatment. Hyssop is known to be safe in low doses with a couple of exceptions. As it's packed with ketones, avoid pregnancy because the herb may cause uterine distress or trigger menstruation. If you're prone to seizures, avoid taking this herb since it might spur their onset or hcighten them.

4.14 Lavender Herb

Lavender is no one-hit-wonder. A powerfully, in fact, it's one of the few essential oils which herbalists recommend applying directly to the skin for healing cuts, wounds, scrapes, and bruises with zero side effects. In ancient times, a pound of lavender blossoms would set you back about a month's salary if you're a farmworker. The Greeks discovered early that crushed and properly treated lavender could release a relaxing fume when burned. Later it was used for smoking, mummifying, and perfuming. French chemist René-Maurice Gatehouses, who coined the term aromatherapy, endured terrible burns after a laboratory explosion. In a last-ditch effort at recovery, he rubbed his traces with lavender essential oils, which sped healing and left his skin almost scar-free. A recurrent, lavender is a hardy plant ready to grow nearly anywhere. In reality, you've likely noticed it growing in meadows, near roadsides, and in lush, mountainous areas. While its typical habitat makes it appropriate for Zones 5 to 8, give this herb some sunlight, warmth, and moist, well-drained dirt, and it is a happy camper.

4.15 Yarrow Achillea millefleur

Yarrow is one of the fascinating herbs. You will find it. Said for a cure-all, it's been widely used across the planet for centuries in many different modalities and civilizations. It is best known for

Each type of oil has its benefits and pitfalls. These applications will have to be dealt with at a recipe by recipe mode in considerably more detail than is covered in this publication.

Each includes its attributes, and these distinctive properties permit their applications to change from fast absorbed transdermal applications to suppositories. Each has different uses that rely on varying temperature and their respective active elements. A fantastic example could be Aloe. Aloe is best used fresh, but they also create wonderful houseplants and may come in rather handy when required. Whenever using a fresh herb, it's always suggested that a bit of it be set on the tongue for many minutes, and at least an hour ought to pass before utilizing it as a curative herb. It will allow time to allow the consumer to make sure he isn't allergic to the herb. Although virtually all herbs used have no or minimal toxicity, allergies don't exist. It's advisable to ensure one isn't allergic to the herb before using it for medicinal purposes. A flavor of this herb when it's chosen is almost always a fantastic idea anyway. With experience, you'll have the ability to tell if the plant is at its peak and start to become conscious of the subtle changes which happen when a plant is at its summit for herbal usage. It is going to immediately become evident that all herbs don't have a nice flavor or feel. I don't enjoy the flavor of several medicinal herbs. However, I will tell you when the actives are in their summit by this simple tasting method.

3.6 Essential Tools & Instruments

A few of those tools are everyday things a Well-stocked kitchen might already have—others you might not have noticed or used before. In any event, if you would like to create more of your herbal teas, tinctures, salves, or more in your home, here are a couple of essential tools each herbalist should inventory in your kitchen.

➤ **Potato Ricer**

Hands down, the BEST herbal tool you can own is a potato ricer. Yes, you read that correctly. Have you ever seen a tincture press? They are quite expensive! A potato ricer will do the same thing for you! Use this when you're straining every tincture or infused oil. It will get every last drop of liquid out of your herbs.

➤ **Spice Grinder**

I love to keep my herbs whole as long as Potential and then grind them after I am prepared to use them. It keeps them clean longer and retains many of their medicinal properties. Herbal powders oxidize and lose their effectiveness speedily. Maintain a spice grinder available and procedure your herbs as you need them for the very best taste and medicine.

➤ **Scissors & Baskets**

First things first, you Require a basket to Carry your herbs and scissors to crop them with. I love to locate baskets in thrift shops, and I search for them each time I see one. Any basket with a handle will do. You also require high-quality scissors to harvest herbs as a few stalks are relatively thick. This pair is quite sturdy, comfortable and the blades can be sharpened as necessary.

> **Pleasing Mesh Sieve**

One of my most used herbal tools is my fine mesh sieves. I have three different sizes, in a set like this one, and I use all of them all the time! I am continually straining something in the kitchen, and I use these sieves for it all. The largest one is perfect for pulling tinctures or infused oils with my potato ricer.

> **Mortar and Pestle**

A mortar and pestle are so beautiful and decorative! They work well to grind your herbs coarsely, and did I say beautiful? It's fun to use them! Alternatively, you can use a spice grinder, but I love my mortar and pestle set.

> **Kitchen Scale**

It's essential to consider your ingredients for Some herbal recipes, namely, tinctures and teas. Sometimes you need those exact Measurements to ensure you can make the tea

4.2 Mountain Arnica

Plant some arnica in your garden, and you're going to have this perennial for two springs. You will realize this medicinal attractiveness due to its glowing yellow, daisy-like appearance and around, hairy stalks. Through its active ingredients are primarily regarded as analgesic and anti-inflammatory, some herbalists use it as an antibiotic, especially for topical skin ailments. It was revered since the 1600s for its pain-relieving prowess. German philosopher Goethe is rumored to have smoked its leaves and drank its tea to ease chest discomfort. Many studies have recently concluded that the herb is effective for relieving muscle pain because of rigorous exercise. In reality, a 2003 study published in Homeopathy revealed it worked better than the placebo for treating muscular soreness on runners who just finished a 26.2-mile marathon. Arnica is usually considered toxic in amounts more significant than what you'd see in cosmetics or food. In reality, the amount you discover in herbal or homeopathic remedies are generally so diluted they are deemed secure. Do not use on broken skin, before or after the operation (it increases flow), or when you have digestive conditions. It's considered unsafe to inhale or use as aromatherapy.

4.3 Black Cohosh Plants

Black cohosh will be your best friend if you experience painful or uncomfortable menopausal or PMS symptoms. The mixture of its ingredients--tannins, resins, fatty acids, 27-deoxyactein, isoflavones, triterpene glycosides, and formononetin--mimic the hormone estrogen and has been clinically shown to alleviate congestion, cramps, bloating, mood swings, depression, and much more. North American Indians used black cohosh to treat gynecological conditions, kidney problems, malaria, snake bites, coughs, and colds. Herbalists have since primarily focused on women's pain related to the uterus, ovaries, infertility, and labor pains. At the same time, it's also used in alternative remedies for neurological and lung ailments. Researchers urge not to take black cohosh if you are breastfeeding, pregnant, diagnosed with breast cancer, or possess hormone-sensitive problems that could be triggered by the herb, which stimulates estrogen in the body. Should you take the herb internally, take a rest after one year. Also, stop if you are experiencing unwanted effects like upset stomach, headaches, cramps, weight gain, spotting, or bleeding between menstrual periods. It thrives in moist, organic grime and must undergo a completely warm and cold cycle to heat until the seeds germinate. Ensure success by putting mature seeds in autumn; therefore, it experiences the process and up your odds of growing throughout its first spring.

4.4 Dandelion Herb

Half the world loves this plant, using it for medication and dining on it daily. The other half was trying to ruin it with chemical warfare because of the 1940s. However, dandelion's tenacity a part of its attractiveness and, perhaps, has something to do with its medicinal properties. The roots are superior liver tonic and will help relieve poor digestion and lower bowel complaints. The leaves are a mild diuretic used to treat water retention and kidney its dual nature. For instance, it triggers bleeding and stops bleeding. It makes sense because yarrow, like spearmint, is known to be "amphoteric," meaning it moves to the place in or on your body where it's needed. At the same time, it's soothing and stimulating, depending on the patient's needs. Even more intriguing, it works almost immediately, significantly if reducing swelling or stopping bleeding, also carries down high fevers in record time (that is because it's also diaphoretic and triggers sweating!).

Yarrow is named after Achilles, the Greek Trojan War pioneer, who used it during battle. He jumped his warriors' feet from the herb to stop bleeding and cure their wounds more quickly. Yarrow is one of our most versatile and healing plants, beloved and respected by people using it. A gorgeous roadside weed, yarrow is best recognized by its creamy white flowers that bloom in clusters atop a stem throughout the summertime. Yarrow blossoms and leaves are exceptional diaphoretics (promote sweating). Diaphoretics such as yarrow are often suggested to reduce a fever by helping someone produce sweat. Yarrow is also a very useful first-aid remedy used to prevent bleeding internally and externally. It can be applied externally as a poultice or wash or taken internally as a tea or tincture. It is also an effective treatment for stomach and menstrual cramps and muscle spasms. If that is not enough, yarrow also has beneficial effects on the lungs and heart. Yarrow can be prepared as an infusion, tinctures nicely, and can be encapsulated. It will make a bitter extract, so combine it with tastier herbs for use as a digestive aid and diaphoretic. The dried, powdered leaves and flowers are helpful first aid items for disinfecting wounds and assisting cuts in preventing bleeding. A pinch of the powder can be placed in the nose to stop a nosebleed.

4.16 Burdock Arctium

If you've had Japanese takeout recently, Chances are you've had burdock root. Not only does it taste great, but it's also loaded with anti-inflammatory, antioxidant, anticancer, antibacterial, and other healing features. New studies have even shown that it may be prebiotic, which encourages the growth of beneficial bacteria in your intestines and keeps you healthy in cold and flu season. If you create it like a side dish in your home, gourmets and herbalists will tell you two things: Leave the skin--it's got enormous nutrients, and soak the roots for 15 to 20 minutes before broiling, boiling, or sautéing to shed its bitter, muddy notes. Do not worry; it's tastier than it seems. Most recently, burdock had its 15 minutes of fame in the '90s with the explosion of Velcro. George de Mistral created the cloth fastening device in 1948 after going on a hiking trip, and his dog and locating burdock burrs stuck on his clothes and his best buddy's fur. Burdock is one of those aggressive, impossible-to-destroy weeds you have likely tried to ruin if you have a garden. In other words, before you learned about its incredible healing possible. A real survivor, this herb grows on just about any dirt from dry to rocky to damp, survives freezes and droughts, also doesn't have a taste about the sun.

4.17 Licorice or Licorice

The Actual herb (instead of the candies) is Naturally sweet--50 times sweeter than sugar, actually --and chock full of healing chemicals. Even more shocking, the ingredient which produces licorice so sweet (glycyrrhizin acid) is one of the root's secret weapons thanks to its anti-inflammatory, antiviral, and anti-arthritic advantages that mimic hydrocortisone and corticosteroids from the body. While much of licorice's benefits are still considered lore--though the herb has been used extensively throughout Europe and Asia for centuries--an injectable form of the plant was revealed in a clinical trial to effectively fight hepatitis C. Herbalists state that ginger falls into the group of "Mediterranean plant." In other words, it enjoys full sunlight, higher warmth, and sandy to partially sandy soil. If you are raising this herb indoors, be aware that you will want about three years until it is medicinally prepared to use if you take it from seed to harvest. The practical and delicious attributes of licorice help make it one of the most crucial herbal remedies. It is used for many situations, including bronchial congestion, sore throat, coughs, and effective antifungal medication for shingles, herpes, and other viral infections. Using its exceptional mucilaginous properties, licorice can heal the respiratory tract and digestive tract's inflammation and be soothing and healing to nausea. It is excellent for toning the endocrine system also can be a particular herbal remedy for adrenal exhaustion. In traditional Chinese medicine, licorice is regarded as a "superior medicine" and is used as a harmonizer in many formulas. Licorice is very sweet and must be blended with other herbs to be more palatable. Though most men and women enjoy the flavor and taste of licorice, several individuals have a strong aversion. It can be produced into a wash or poultice for viral diseases such as herpes and shingles as a tea. For adrenal exhaustion, tiredness, and fatigue, drink 2 to 3 cups of licorice tea a day, blended with additional endocrine tonic herbs like wild yam, sarsaparilla, burdock root, and sassafras. For sore throats, prepare ginger for a cough syrup; mix it with pleurisy root and elecampane for deep-seated bronchial inflammation, and blend it with marshmallow root for digestive inflammation and ulcers.

4.18 Mullein Verbascum

An expectorant and antispasmodic, though some researchers have questioned its effectiveness as an antibacterial, others in Clemson University discovered mullein to successfully fight bacteria like Staphylococcus aureus, Staphylococcus epidermis, E. coli, and pneumonia. Another European plant initially considered ward off evil spirits; this specific herb was considered among the 23 most potent healers in Egyptian medication. Mullein, a biennial, makes a great addition to any backyard --it's appealing and lures in both bees and birds. Once it thrives in Zones 3 to 8, it's pretty happy everywhere you plant it. If you're into nature walks or outside exploration, you've likely seen it growing in the wild in areas, by streams, in woods, or adjacent to highways. (It's easy to see, given its own skinny, stalk-like stem and seven-foot stature.) It is among my favorite wayside weeds. It is always so stately, sometimes sending its flowering stalk several feet high into the sky. That stalk is filled with beautiful, fragrant yellow blossoms that produce the very best oil for ear infections. The flowers both fight the disease and relieve the pain. The elongated fuzzy leaves that form a rosette at the base of this plant are used for hundreds of years in cough formulas and can be used for all manner of respiratory and bronchial asthma and infections. The leaves are also excellent for curing vaginal imbalances and are suggested whenever there's glandular swelling. Mullein leaves and flowers may be utilized in capsule, tea, and tincture form. For bronchial congestion, colds, and coughs, combine the leaves with coltsfoot leaves and peppermint and prepare tea. To fight ear infections, prepare a solar infused oil in the blossoms, using olive oil.

4.19 Eucalyptus Gum Trees

Eucalyptus gets its title from its healthy Active ingredient, eucalyptol, which constitutes about 70 percent of its compounds. It has significant anti-inflammatory, antiseptic, antiseptic, antiviral, decongestant, and antimicrobial properties. Its woodsy oils create a potent aromatherapy instrument for balancing and stimulating the mind, body, and emotions and treating viral ailments and respiratory ailments. Utilizing the herb for steam inhalation can also be excellent for clearing out the lungs, starting nasal passages, and treating sinuses. With over 300 species and 700 unique varieties, eucalyptus is a favorite among healers for centuries. Aborigines used it to disinfect wounds, lessen pain, and push fevers. Taken at the onset of colds, fever, flu, sinusitis, bronchitis, or other ailments, it's said to accelerate healing and shorten sickness. Eucalyptus must be diluted before applying topically to the skin. If you have diabetes, note that eucalyptus Growing chamomile indoors is easy and rather ordinary. It requires full sun and well-drained soil. If you're planting outside, heads up, this tree won't achieve its maximum height possible unless you live in a warm climate.

4.20 Rosehips Rose Haw

While this beautiful red fruit is revered for its vitamin C content, it is like a multivitamin grown to a tree due to vitamins A, D, E, essential fatty acids, and antioxidant-rich flavonoids. Rosehips are used to flavor teas and jellies, and it is a good thing for the immune system. While fresh rosehips constitute a significant source of vitamin C, dried rosehips? Not so much. The act of drying the plant zaps a fantastic piece of its C content.

4.21 Rosemary

Rosemary is not only for seasoning lamb anymore. This broadly studied herb includes an active ingredient known as carnosol acid demonstrated in scientific studies to get severe protective effects in mind. A recent analysis published in the Journal of Neurochemistry reveals that it protects brain cells from free radicals and might be employed to take care of neurodegenerative ailments like Parkinson's, Alzheimer's, and stroke. Researchers consider continuing studies to demonstrate the herb for effective anti-aging treatment due to its capacity to prevent disease, slow aging, and encourage the nervous system. The mint family (along with ginger, oregano, and lavender) has been used for everything from petrol relief and toothaches to hair loss and memory reduction. From the nineteenth century, physicians burnt rosemary in their ill chambers to disinfect the recovery area and kill germs. In reality, it will not survive a freeze. It is often safest to maintain the herb inside in a brightly sunny place with steady temperatures and soil dampness control.

4.22 Sage Herb

While There Are Lots of Kinds of sage, Salvia Officinalis has become the most useful variety quickly to your herbal medication kit. Even though there are lots of distinct sorts of sage inside precisely the same household, they have various advantages and uses. This specific blossom --analcime sage"--is widely utilized in aromatherapy in addition to for wounds, diseases, and cleansing solutions because of the antibacterial chemicals. In ancient Roman and Greek times, royalty downed countless lavender teacups, believing it had been a fountain of youth types. During that same period, the herb has been used both as a meat preservative and a memory booster. In reality, rosemary was utilized throughout the Black Death to fight against the illness. It appears these early civilizations were on something. Research has shown the herb to boost memory and fight against Alzheimer's disease.

4.23 Self-Heal Herb

A popular in skincare lines due to its high vitamin C, vitamin K, thiamine, and tannins material, self-heal is popularly famous for its antiseptic, antibacterial, and anti-inflammatory advantages. It's rooted in gourmet circles too: Self-heal's leaves and stalks (dried or fresh) are the key ingredients on your next farm-to-table gourmet or salad soup. Its fabulous purple blossoms brighten any bowl of greens with no guests using Its title "self-heal" stems from the fact that at once, this superb herb has been regarded as a panacea. Its ingredient profile includes cancer preventative, STD (sexually transmitted disease) remedies, and antioxidants proven to prevent cardiovascular disease and improve immunity. It is required to enhance mood from a psychological standpoint, increase energy levels, balance hormones, and wake self-confidence and life force. In reality, it's one of those only herbal essences created to a skin lotion made to reinforce self-health and self-sustenance.

4.24 Thyme Herb

You are packed with natural recovery Stash this herb on your medication kit to resist everything from colds and influenza symptoms to baldness and fantastic breath. As you would not expect to get this herb on your skincare regimen, its antibacterial, antibacterial, antifungal, and astringent qualities make it a shoo-in for curing demanding acne, preventing blemishes, toning and tightening skin, and deodorizing head. Not bad for something you generally book for herbs de Provence. If saltwater could speak, it would let you know about how it was utilized by the Egyptians to mummify the dead or the way the Greeks gave it into its warriors to reinforce courage. As it is antiseptic, thyme was used by physicians to wash wounds.

4.25 Witch Hazel Hamamelidaceous

The anti-inflammatory power of the wild tree. Great for healing sunburn, bug bites, and bruises, and you are going to discover that it's an essential addition to backpacks and camping equipment. Witch hazel is equally as popular in attractiveness circles. Its eye drops and astringent properties make it a superb component in anti-aging skincare formulas and nourishing spa treatments. Add it into a cotton ball for everyday usage and then swipe face to fight acne, decrease fine lines and wrinkles, and shrink pores and remove makeup. At one stage, the tree has been known as a "water witch" because its branches have been used to find underground mineral and water resources. Since they blossom in sunlight, they are often planted by men and women who require a visual psychological increase or aromatherapeutic pick-me-up through the long winter season. A North American tree using all the witchy habit of flowering in winter after the rest of the shrubs and trees have dropped their leaves, witch hazel is a renowned astringent tonic herb. The inner bark of this shrub is a powerful pain reliever and astringent. It's considered to act on the lymph system to stop inflammation and bleeding, both externally and internally. It's beneficial for digestive bleeding, hemorrhoids, varicose veins, as well as nausea.

Additionally, it is suggested to prevent bleeding of the lungs and nose. Witch hazel can be made into a tincture or salve and employed externally as an astringent, disinfectant scrub.

Additionally, it produces a fantastic cleaner for distressed skin. It's still easy to locate witch hazel extract in pharmacies, as well as some grocery stores. Just be sure that it's pure distilled witch hazel produced from the bark of Hamamelis virginiana.

4.26 Wild yam

Wild yam has an Intricate activity Physically And can be used for several essential functions. It's the primary source material for both steroid manufacturing and is a hormone stimulant. It hastens the endocrine glands' process and assists in the everyday use of both genders' reproductive system. It's been used as a treatment for the menstrual disorder, to stimulate the digestion and liver, and to increase fertility in women that are progesterone deficient. Wild yam additionally has nervine and antispasmodic properties. Also, it's a superb treatment for soothing muscle cramps, colic, and uterine pain. It's also beneficial for relieving liver blockage and normalizing gut function. Use wild yam in formulations for the reproductive system of both women and men.

Additionally, it can be made in teas, tinctures, and capsules. It's seriously depleted in its typical habitat. Buy only from cultivated sources.

4.27 White oak Herb

White walnut Herb Bark is a strong astringent and disinfectant. The high tannin content from the bark, leaves, and gall creates the white walnut incredibly helpful for treating asthma, dysentery, and migraines. It may be ready as an astringent, antiseptic wash for wounds, poison oak, and poison ivy. It's also employed as a gargle for sore throats and gum and tooth diseases, as a douche for leukorrhea, and a wash or poultice for varicose veins. The white pine's inner bark is often used, but the leaves and gall can also be full of tannins and quite astringent. It's usually made into a decoction for internal functions and an antiseptic ointment for outside parts. White pine bark also tinctures nicely and can be found in formulations for tooth/gum ailments, sore throats, and skin ailments like poison oak and poison ivy.

4.28 Astragalus Herb

Called "the young individual's ginseng," astragalus reinforces the immune system also helps reconstruct the bone marrow book that regenerates the body's protective shield. It's a superior tonic herb that is used in treating chronic imbalances. It's also handy for regulating the metabolism of dietary sugars, and consequently, it's helpful for individuals with diabetes. Astragalus is best utilized in tea for long-term illness, reduced energy, and encouraging and building profound immune power. Astragalus may also be used in capsule form. Or just eat it as is placing a complete root or two at a kettle of soup and simmer for many hours, or even chew on it just like a licorice stick; it is quite yummy.

4.29 Biennial Plants

Farmers and a boon to herbalists. It's just the best herb to the skin and may be used internally and externally for psoriasis, eczema, psoriasis, as well as other skin-related imbalances. It's a superior tonic herb for the liver. Its pleasant flavor is frequently formulated with additional less yummy "liver " Burdock creates a fine-tasting tea teenager with problem skin may try it mixed with juice or other herbal teas. Decoct the origin and function of meals as a digestive aid. The seeds are frequently utilized in lotions for skin.

4.30 Cayenne Pepper Capsicum Annuum

Cayenne is loved worldwide, together with, and it is somewhat deserving of all of the attention it gets. Not only is a fantastic fired-up culinary herb used in all types of dishes globally, but it's also a highly valued medicinal plant. It functions as a catalyst into the system, stimulating the body's natural defense mechanisms. It's antifungal properties and is a superb heating circulatory herb. It's among the very best heart tonics, raising the pulse and toning the muscle. In the end, it's a tremendous carminative, sparking the digestive process and assisting with constipation and congestion. Cayenne may be appropriately used in several formulations (capsules, teas, tinctures, and food preparations) as a catalyst or activity herb. The burning sensation it generates is shallow rather than harmful. Cayenne, though secure, is sexy. A pinch of cayenne in a tincture formulation may overwhelm, along with a more or grain within an herbal pill, may send one to the ceiling! Use with care and only in little quantities. Always wash your hands well with soap and warm water (or vegetable oil or lotion) after working using saltwater not to move it to your eye.

4.31 Raspberry Herb

Measure apart chia, raspberry leaves and seeds Are thought of as among the trendiest new superfoods around. It is no surprise. Beauty fans are fairly psyched about its capacity to eliminate acne scars, treat and prevent breakouts, reduce wrinkles, smooth skin surface, and even skin tone. Blackberry foliage makes an equally excellent (and antioxidant-rich) substitution. Raspberry is widely known for its advantages of encouraging pregnancy, labor, and delivery. Many civilizations have used it to deal with a vast selection of ailments, such as hypertension, kidney disorders, and illnesses. Topically, its leaves are a very potent disinfectant and are applied to wounds to accelerate recovery. Raspberry bushes flourish in Zones 3 to 9 in regions with complete sunshine, fertile, well-drained dirt, and decent airflow. Do not plant near a place that develops or is used to create tomatoes, potatoes, peppers, eggplants, bramble berries, or roses, which may cause harmful diseases that could attack and destroy the fruit.

4.32 Slippery Elm

Slippery elms, together with other elm trees, partly because of their low prices and slow-growing character, making their inhabitants slow to replenish. It's possible to discover little and full-grown trees offered in specific nurseries in addition to online because their bark remains in demand. Most herbalists substitute marshmallows in recipes whenever permitted or readily available. A wholesome tree could top 60 feet tall. What is coveted for medicinal usage is the bark in the branches. Slippery elm is famed because of its "mucilaginous" consistency, meaning that the thick, gooey texture inherent in certain crops. Together with its natural anti-inflammatory, anti-irritant features, this viscosity makes it a soothing, nourishing ingredient in contemporary skincare lines. Back in the day, Native Americans utilized to soak slippery elm bark, cover wounds and permit it to dry over the wounded area since the bark exerts its therapeutic compounds to the skin.

4.33 Chaste Tree Herb

Chaste tree, a tree native to the Mediterranean Area, has been used by Europeans since early times. It's among the main herbs for nourishing and feeding both women and men's reproductive organs and is incredibly valuable in restoring energy and overall tone into the female system. (While the chaste tree is an essential herb for many women, it does not work for everybody; listen when first using it to see whether it is the best option for you.) Many men and women use it to boost their sexual energy, even though there's some controversy regarding whether it arouses or depresses sexual appetite. I find it amphoteric inactivity, meaning it wakes or pushes determined by what your body requires while still addressing the imbalance's origin. Chaste tree berries taste and look somewhat like black pepper. Even though they may be vaporized in tea, they are ordinarily utilized in tincture or capsule form. They may also be placed into a pepper grinder, also used like pepper.

4.34 Cleavers Herb

Often found growing near chickweed; they appear to relish the identical habitat. And both are usually combined in formulas too. The two cleavers and chickweed are gentle, secure diuretics, and are both utilized to tone and soothe irritations of the kidneys and urinary tract. Additionally, cleavers are a superb lymphatic cleanser and is frequently used as a safe, effective treatment for swollen glands, tonsillitis, and several tumors. Prepare in precisely the same manner as chickweed.

4.35 Coltsfoot Herb

Coltsfoot is a frequent weed found growing along roadsides, ditches, and streams all over the USA. We frequently confuse it with dandelion, as the blossoms are alike. However, coltsfoot blossoms at the first aspect of spring, before the big, curved leaves appear.

4.36 Comfrey Herb

Full of allantoin and profoundly recovery, Comfrey is widely utilized in calming poultices, salves, and lotions. It eases and activates the healing of tissue. It's absolutely among the best herbs for torn ligaments, bruises, strains, and other harm to the joints or bones. The origin and the foliage have comparable properties; the head is more powerful; the vegetation is much more palatable. Utilize them both in salves and lotions. The origin is decocted, the foliage is infused. Much like coltsfoot, studies many years ago discovered traces of PLAs in comfrey. The classes were not conclusive, and that I, personally, together with several other herbalists, continue to use comfrey. However, I do not use it in formulations intended for internal usage by others. You may decide for yourself if you feel comfortable eating comfrey. But comfrey is safe to use for outside functions; everybody agrees with it!

4.37 Cornsilk Herb

The corn silk (flower pistils) has been utilized as a goat tonic. It can excite and wash urinary passages while soothing inflammation. It's among the best herbs for counteracting bed-wetting and incontinence. Corn silk can be surprisingly flavorful, tasting somewhat like fresh corn on the cob. Use as a tea throughout the day to reinforce the urinary system. Take corn silk for a tincture at night to help avoid bed-wetting. Other remedies, such as Kegel exercises, should be utilized together with corn silk for the treatment to be effective.

4.38 Echinacea Herb

Best immune-enhancing herbs, which we all know of and among the main herbs of the time. Though exceptionally successful, it's not known to have any side effects or residual buildup within the body. It's also a superb herb for the lymphatics. Though powerful and influential, it's 100-percent secure, even for young kids and the elderly. Take echinacea in regular tiny doses in tea or tincture form to improve immunity at the very first indication of a cold or influenza. It's also practical for bronchial diseases as a tea or tincture. Use as a spray to get sore throats. For sore mouth and gums discomfort, create a mouthwash in the root, using peppermint or spearmint essential oil to taste it.

4.39 Geranium Crane's-bill

Geranium's mother nation is South Africa, but it's been used worldwide for many years to resist infections, migraines, migraines, and much more. A potent astringent, it's famous for cleaning, opening, and diminishing the size of your pores (a wonder must-have for young skin). You'll find it from tonics, toners, skin lotions, serums, and lotions. Additionally, a mood booster, add it into a diffuser in your workplace or close to your tub to soften spirits and fight stress. Herbalists (as well as centuries of anecdotal proof from physicians and nurses) say it is well worth adding to your arsenal of treatments to its anti-inflammatory, antifungal, and antibacterial properties. Early settlers to North America used it for stomach disorders such as nausea, cramps, and gastrointestinal disorders in addition to sexually transmitted diseases (STDs) and killing warts. A famous disease fighter, you would find geranium in treatments for vaginal infections, menstrual flow, toothaches, as well as acute issues such as typhoid fever. Geraniums are relatively easy to develop, capable of withstanding an assortment of harsh conditions like heat or drought. Their ideal situation is full sun, hot temps, and a covered place, making it suitable for a windowsill inside.

4.40 Elder Herb

You'll discover this yummy product in many pharmacies in addition to natural food shops throughout Europe. In the USA, elderberry syrup and tincture are popular remedies for cold and influenza germs, though you're more inclined to locate them in pill and organic food shops than in pharmacies. Both the berries and blossoms are strong diaphoretics: by causing sweat, and they reduce fevers. Elder has strong immune-enhancing and antibacterial properties as well and can be much better when combined with echinacea. Elderberries make a number of the greatest syrups and perfumes you will ever taste. Each summer, I gather the significant, aromatic horizontal clusters of elder blossoms and make elderflower fritters a special summer treat.

There are a couple of distinct varieties of elder which grow in the USA. People who have blueberries are safe to consume, though most men and women agree that it is best not to eat the fruit uncooked to cook, tender, or tincture it. The berries of red-green, a little tree that grows in high elevations and appears like the blue-green, except its vivid red fruit, aren't edible. Do not eat red elderberries!

4.41 Chickweed Herb

Chickweed can be seen globally in moist, cultivated Soil and is often regarded as a weed. It's frequently utilized in salves and poultices for migraines and other skin irritations. It's a mild diuretic and can be suggested for water retention. Additionally, chickweed is a treasure trove of nutrients, such as potassium, calcium, and iron. They may also be juiced; they are incredibly useful, mixed with lemon juice. A mild infusion of chickweed is incredibly soothing. This herb does not dry or store well, so to conserve it for future usage, consider tincturing a number of the following crop of chickweed that pops in your backyard. As opposed to seeing it as a bud, see it because of the recovery, tender, and stubborn little plant.

4.42 Oregon Grape Mahonia Auditorium

The origins of the Gorgeous holly-like plant Are gaining popularity since they contain berberine, a compound like the active ingredient in goldenseal. Oregon grape root is used in goldenseal to help avoid overharvesting of the herb; however, Oregon grape is also a slow-growing perennial using a restricted growing range. Much like goldenseal, Oregon grape root is used both externally and internally to combat infections. It's exceptional anti-inflammatory, antiseptic, and antibacterial properties. It's frequently utilized in formulations to encourage liver wellbeing and digestive troubles.

Additionally, it is an essential herb for skin issues like eczema, psoriasis, eczema, and psoriasis. A decoction of the root may be utilized as a topical scrub for diseases. Whether picking yourself or buying it from retailers, then take care to encourage sustainable practices that restrict the potential of overharvesting Oregon grape root. Though often successful where it's located rising, Oregon grape has a restricted selection. If wild inhabitants appear to be diminishing, we might determine that this herb be utilized from just cultivated resources, leaving the uncontrolled stands to grow.

4.43 Elecampane Elf dock

You'll discover this yummy product in many pharmacies in addition to natural food shops throughout Europe. In the USA, elderberry syrup and tincture are popular remedies for cold and influenza germs, though you're more inclined to locate them in pill and organic food shops than in pharmacies. Both the berries and blossoms are strong diaphoretics: by causing sweat, and they reduce fevers. Elder has strong immune-enhancing and antibacterial properties as well and can be much better when combined with echinacea. Elderberries make a number of the greatest syrups and perfumes you will ever taste. Each summer, I gather the significant, aromatic horizontal clusters of elder blossoms and make elderflower fritters a special summer treat. There are a couple of distinct varieties of elder which grow in the USA. People who have blueberries are safe to consume, though most men and women agree that it is best not to consume the fruit raw but to cook, dry, or tincture it. The berries of red-green, a little tree that grows in high elevations and appears like the blue-green, except its vivid red fruit, aren't edible. Do not eat red elderberries!

4.44 Fennel Herb

A Favorite carminative and digestive help, Fennel was utilized by the ancient Greek doctors to get all manner of gastrointestinal troubles and to increase and enhance blood flow in nursing mothers. It's a powerful antacid, both excess polyunsaturated acid in the stomach and lowering uric acid in the joints, thus helping to fight inflammation. They may also be used to ease colic. With their licorice-like taste, fennel seeds are rather yummy and are frequently blended with other flavorful herbs to create formulations more palatable. They may be prepared as a tea to ease colic, enhance digestion, and expel gas in the system. (Recall, however, the gasoline does not evaporate but is discharged, which means you might be tooting somewhat!) Nursing mothers can drink 2-3 cups of fennel tea every day to increase the stream of your milk. Fennel tea also creates a soothing scrub for inflammation and soreness in the uterus. It may be used with infection-fighting herbs such as goldenseal to treat conjunctivitis and other eye ailments. (Recall, however, breed the fennel tea nicely to not get any herb particles on your eyes).

4.45 Feverfew Tanacetum parthenium L.
This Frequent garden flower comes with an outstanding Standing for treating migraines. Recent clinical studies have proved it also alleviates inflammation and stress-related stress. As it's relatively sour, I generally unite feverfew with lavender and California poppy to create a tincture. As a migraine preventative, just take 1/2 into one teaspoon of the tincture two to 3 times per day for five days, rest for two days, then repeat the cycle. Feverfew is best for treating migraines when taken over 2-3 months, even though it's also going to relieve acute migraine symptoms when taken at the earliest signs of a migraine. Although it's ideal for tincturing the herb brand new, I have discovered that high quality, correctly dried feverfew functions too.

4.46 Ginkgo Biloba
Ginkgo Biloba Slow-growing large perennial shrub that can live into a rugged old era. The only survivor of the earliest known tree

genus, Ginkgoaceae, dates back over 200 million years. And possibly it's standing as a veritable living fossil account because of its outstanding ability to help with recall and memory. Ginkgo functions as a "brain food" and is an excellent memory aid. Additionally, it enhances energy and enhances circulation. I propose ginkgo as a regular tonic herb for anybody experiencing memory loss or "brain exhaustion " Recently, it's been proven to stop the development of Alzheimer's disease if administered in therapeutic dosages (i.e., standardized extracts) within a period. Ginkgo has to be used with consistency for many weeks until you will find its advantages. Generally speaking, ginkgo is thriving as a tea, a tincture, or capsules to fortify the brain and flow. Due to its effects on the blood and circulatory system, ginkgo should be stopped for two weeks before and after the operation. Even though it is not usually a problem in these instances, it is much better to err on the side of care.

4.47 Yellow dock Herb

This abundant crazy weed of gardens, areas, and roadsides is very possibly among the very best herbs for the whole digestive tract, including the liver. The massive taproot is full of anthraquinones, which possess a laxative activity. Though yellow dock root does not contain much iron, it assists in the assimilation and distribution of iron in our bodies, making it especially helpful for anyone who has low iron. It's among the very best herbs for nausea and fatigue brought on by low iron levels. The origin is an excellent help for slow digestion and constipation. The chemical components are easily extracted utilizing a water decoction and from alcohol. Yellow dock creates a somewhat bitter decoction; therefore, it's best formulated with much more yummy herbs. The tincture is excellent for the liver, liver, and digestion. It may be added to formulations because of its analgesic properties. It creates an iron-rich syrup, incorporating other iron-rich herbs like nettle, chickweed, dandelion leaves, and root.

4.48 Goldenseal Herb

It is quite possibly among the very Valuable and useful plants of North America. Especially effective at curing mucous membranes, goldenseal is employed in cleaning washes for your eye, as a douche for diseases (cautious: it may be too drying to your vagina if not appropriately formulated), in mouthwashes for sore mouths and mouths, and at the topical treatment for psoriasis and psoriasis. It contains antifungal, antifungal, and antiseptic properties and is frequently combined with additional infection-fighting herbs to help fight infections and ward off colds and flu cases. Goldenseal is quite bitter and is commonly utilized as a bitter tonic and digestive aid. The origin is infused (maybe not decocted) as a sour tea, which may be used as a mouthwash for gum diseases and as a topical wash for cuts. Blend the herb with echinacea to help fight infections and colds. If used within a period, goldenseal becomes an irritant to the mucous membranes, resulting in inflammation and aggravation. Always rotate its usage (for example, five days on, two days away), nor use it for more than three months at one time.

4.49 Hawthorn Herb

Hawthorn is very possibly the best hub Tonic herb there's. It's been admired and surrounded by legend for centuries and can be employed as a curative plant in each nation it develops in. Hawthorn dilates the veins and arteries, allowing blood to flow more freely by discharging cardiovascular constrictions and blockages. Additionally, it can help maintain wholesome cholesterol levels. As it's regarded as food instead of medicine, it's usually considered safe to use together with heart medicine. But if you are taking any type of pharmaceutical, you should check with your healthcare practitioner before using herbal supplements. Hawthorn is yummy as a tea, syrup, and shake, and it could also be tinctured.

4.50 Hibiscus Flowering Plant

Hibiscus is packed with vitamin C, Bioflavonoids, antioxidants, and many other minerals and vitamins. With its abundant, glowing reddish pigment, it elevates its affinity for the center, and, honestly, it's an excellent heart tonic. The giant tropical blossoms make a brilliant reddish tea that's tasty and sour, with a sweet aftertaste. Hibiscus is frequently formulated with stevia or other sweet herbs to improve its taste. It brightens any tea with its fantastic ruby red color. Consider creating a thick hibiscus syrup and then add it into sparkling water for a yummy punch. Packed with vitamins and minerals, this drink is much superior compared to sugar-loaded soda.

4.51 Marshmallow Herbal

Family, which also has hibiscus and hollyhock. It's a particularly benevolent household; it does not have any poisonous members, and several of those "malls" are utilized for food and medication. Marshmallow is among the most famous members of the family. The Romans believed its origin for a yummy vegetable, and also, the candy leaves were considered a culinary cure one of many ancient civilizations. Early leaders in the USA boiled the powdered root with glucose to produce a sweet confection, which later morphed into the marshmallow we understand today. (Regrettably, the new candy is devoid of this herb for which it's named.) A soothing, mucilaginous herb, marshmallow creates a yummy tea for sore throats, respiratory distress, and gastrointestinal troubles. It's excellent for helping to soothe and treat ailments and other inflammatory conditions.

Additionally, it is especially beneficial for treating urinary tract infections and urinary problems, and in such instances, it's often combined with other sinus tonics like chickweed and cleavers. The powdered root or foliage may be blended to a paste with water for soothing skin irritations. Marshmallow and oatmeal may also be utilized in the bath for a gentle clean. Marshmallow may be tinctured, but its mucilaginous components are more soluble in water than in alcohol. Therefore, water preparations like tea and syrup are more powerful.

4.52 Milk Thistle Herb

The seeds of the large wild thistle have been Nature's most significant help for damaged liver tissue. It directly stimulates liver functioning and rebuilds damaged liver cells. Its tonifying activities make it a valuable part of cleansing applications and an essential nutritional supplement for individuals whose livers are compromised by illness, hepatitis, or alcoholism. Milk thistle seed can also be valuable for the gallbladder as well as the kidneys. The hard-black sources ought to be ground so the chemical components can be quickly drawn out. Utilize the floor seeds into tinctures or tea, or scatter them straight on food.

4.53 Motherwort Leonurus Cardiac

Properties for ladies, particularly for menopausal women, but it is equally valuable as a heart tonic. It's an excellent tonic for strengthening and nourishing the heart and its blood vessels. It's appreciated as a remedy for several women's issues, for example, delayed menstruation, uterine cramps related to scanty menses, water retention, and hot flashes and mood swings through menopause. Motherwort grows readily in the backyard. Prepare as an extract flavored with tastier herbs, and drink a few cups per day. Or get ready as a tincture.

4.54 Nettle Herb

often Regarded as a pesky plant by anglers, Nettle is nonetheless appreciated by herbalists worldwide. It's a flavorful wild green when steamed and rich in minerals and vitamins, particularly calcium and iron. It's an age-old treatment for allergies, hay fever, and respiratory ailments. Due to its nutrient density, and notably its bio chelated calcium, nettle is great for kids and is remarkably suggested for growing pains, as soon as their joints and bones ache. A superb reproductive tonic for women and men, nettle is used to relieve the symptoms of PMS and menopause and enhance fertility in both men and women once the infertility is a result of inadequate nutrition. Nettle is also known as a scalp and hair tonic; it is believed to maintain a complete head of healthy hair. It may be utilized to substitute spinach in almost any recipe; however, it should always be nicely cooked; if undercooked, it will sting you! It's also tasty as a tea that may be served many times each day to stop allergies. Nettle is also potent as a tincture.

4.55 Common Oats

Among the best nutritive tonics for your Nervous system, oats are suggested for nervous exhaustion, anxiety, and irritation. The plant's mucilaginous properties allow it to be especially helpful in Treating injury to the myelin sheath surrounding nerve pathways: calcium and protein. Oats are popular partly green until the plant has Turned gold. The milky green shirts and the stalks produce flavorful tea. Among the very best, I believe. Make it powerful and combine with lemon juice. The tea works well for those that are anxious, hyperactive, or worried. You can also use oats to produce a soothing bath for skin discomforts.

5.56 Parsley Herb

This superb garnish Shouldn't be left Slighted across the side of a dish. It might be, in reality, the very nourishing thing on your meal. It'll enhance immunity and can be suggested whenever you're vulnerable to infections. An essential herb for kidney and bladder issues, it's a safe, potent diuretic. Due to this, you shouldn't use parsley in almost any amount when breastfeeding, as it might impede the stream of milk.

4.57 Plantain Herb

Plantain is a Frequent weed found growing Through the temperate areas of the earth. It's frequently the first plant introduced into kids -- place it upon any "boo-boo" or bee sting, and it heals fast. Plantain is one of the very best herbs for poultices of a variety. It is an essential herb for curing blood pressure and blood pressure and is usually employed both externally and internally for this objective. Plantain seeds are full of mucilage and are frequently utilized in laxative blends because of their soothing majority actions. In reality, the psyllium seeds used in Metamucil are generated by a Plantago species. Even though it's frequently described as sour-tasting, plantain is very mild in taste and produces a beautiful extract. It's an excellent herb for poultices for all sorts of skin issues. Additionally, it may be added to foods or used as an herbal first aid powder to get diseases.

4.58 Purple Passionflower

Compounds have calming, sleep-inducing consequences. In reality, the plant has been FDA-approved as an over-the-counter remedy for sleeplessness and sedation. Still, because of insufficient proof regarding its safety and efficacy, it had been pulled out of the market in 1978. If you'd like those effects today, just boil some passionflower tea, stash a few of these fresh herbs beneath your pillow, and allow the Zazas start. Passionflower can likewise be Mother Nature's cure for emotional and mental difficulties associated with stress, mood, anxiety, and associated ailments. One study published in the Journal of Clinical Pharmacy and research revealed the plant extract could handle pressure with no effect on job performance, which exists with the standard pharmaceuticals. Another study demonstrated the herb was successful in reducing stress-related to undergoing an operation. Passionflower is usually considered secure with a couple of exceptions. Avoid if pregnant since the herb was known to cause uterine contractions. Additionally, avoid just two to three weeks before the operation as it might increase anesthesia's effects at the min.

4.59 Red clover Herb

A part of the pea family, crimson clover has Long, slender roots that penetrate several layers of dirt and draw vitamins, minerals, and other components that are usually not located close to the planet's surface. It's famous for its ability to repair nitrogen from the soil, thus functioning as a natural fertilizer. As a medicinal herb, red clover is among the finest respiratory tonics, helpful for young kids in addition to adults, and it's also among the most excellent detoxification herbs. It's but one of those ingredients in conventional anti-cancer formulations like the Horsey formula and Essie tea. Red clover produces flavorful tea. Combine with other herbs like mullein for chronic respiratory difficulty or use nettle for tea to construct the bloodstream and enhance it. The tea or tincture may be used to stop and remove undesirable growths such as tumors, cysts, and fibroids. Hemophiliacs, or individuals with "lean" blood (people who snore heavily or whose blood does not clot easily), shouldn't use red clover. It's referred to as a blood thinner and may encourage prolonged bleeding.

4.60 Red raspberry

Raspberry was cited in Chinese herbal. It was also a beneficial treatment for the North American continent's indigenous peoples, which believed it a nourishing tonic and therapeutic cure for nursing and pregnant women. It's been utilized as a uterine tonic and anabolic supplement since. Raspberry leaves are full of minerals and vitamins, especially iron and calcium. It helps reduce excessive menstruation and is among those exceptional tonics for childbirth and pregnancy. Also, it makes a fantastic mouthwash for sore or infected teeth. It can also be ready in tincture and capsule type and can be made into a yummy syrup.

4.61 Rosehips

use hips contain vitamin C than Any herb, and lots of times that of citrus fruit, even when quantified g by the gram. Rose leaves may also be utilized and are toning and astringent. The beautiful fragrant flowers are used in heart and love potions and several flower essence formulas. Make new rose hips to a vitamin-rich jam or syrup. Rose hips make a flavorful, mild-flavored tea, perfect on a chilly night, sipped with a roaring fire. Or attempt infusing the leaves, buttocks, and blossoms together to get a complete increased tea.

4.62 St. John's Wort

If you have taken any type of road trip Across the USA and Canada, you have likely noticed this herb growing on the side of this street. This herb has been widely studied because of the potent antifungal, antifungal, anti-inflammatory antibacterial and antifungal properties. Its striking buds are most likely best known for their effect on feel-good hormones, such as dopamine, noradrenaline, and dopamine, making it a highly effective antidepressant treatment. (It requires three weeks of constant use because of its mood-boosting consequences to kick.) Hippocrates was a significant fan of St. John's wort and listed its applications in his medical records. It is natively European but has appeared fairly much anyplace. Australia, which currently develops it as an exportable crop, generates 20 percent of its international distribution. Even though it's been used for hundreds of years for neurological impairment and is held in high respect by herbalists, St. John's wort was only recently "rediscovered" because of its antidepressant pursuits. It's effective against moderate depression and appears to raise the spirits used regularly. The gorgeous reddish oil made magically in the merry yellow flowers is an excellent help for injury and is among the most extraordinary topical remedies for bruises, sprains, burns, and injuries of all types. Surely make St. John's Wort Oil; it's among the best medicinal oils. The blossoms and leaves may also be tinctured or prepared as an extract (use roughly 70 percent blossoms to 30 percent leaves).

4.63 Ova ursin Herb

The ground. Its leatherlike leaves are relegated to create tea for bladder and kidney ailments. It's a potent diuretic, astringent, and urinary antiseptic which soothes and soothes urinary passages. Ova ursin is the most successful as an extract for inflammation and disease. A potent infusion mixed with lemon juice can be useful for kidney and bladder ailments. But a decoction will bring a wealthier concentration of tannins along with also the plant's astringent properties.

4.64 Wild cherry Herb

Wild cherry bark is among the very It's a pectoral expectorant, meaning that it will help expel mucus in the lungs, also helps relax and calm the pectoral muscles. It's among the few herbs included from the United States Pharmacopeia and may nevertheless be found in specific industrial cough remedies. It is also a digestive bitter, which enhances digestion and also promotes healthy bowel function. For dry, hacking coughs or spastic coughs that simply will not stop, consider mixing wild cherry bark using valerian root. Made into a tea or tincture, this is a superb combination that will help relax the muscles and expel deep mucus.

4.65 Stevia Herb

Sweeter than sugar is far better for you. It has no calories and does not promote tooth decay. It's suggested for pancreatic ailments and higher glucose. Also, it's a kind of sugar that individuals may easily tolerate. In reality, stevia is used to treat diabetes. Envision a sweetener that's very good for people with diabetes! Though stevia was tested extensively in different nations, it had been banned in the USA on the pretext that its security was unknown. However, when the sugar sector became involved and procured an interest in stevia creation, stevia immediately became legalized, and stevia products started appearing on market shelves. Due to its extreme sweetness, stevia is primarily utilized to improve the taste of teas. But recall, just a tiny amount will do! If you include a pinch a lot into a cup of tea or a recipe, you will ruin the taste. Then I propose making stevia no longer than two percent of the entire formula to control the sweetness.

4.66 Turmeric Flowering Plant

It is among the very best herbs for resistant Wellness and is frequently overlooked due to echinacea's massive popularity. However, it has declared its reputation for centuries because of its immune-enhancing properties and is highly known because of its anti-inflammatory and antibiotic actions. In East Indian medication, it's appreciated as a blood clot and metabolic Remedy. It's used to regulate the menstrual cycle, alleviate cramps, reduce fevers, enhance lousy circulation, and alleviate skin ailments.

4.67 Lemon Balm

Lemon balm scents so stunningly fantastic, you will almost forget it is an extremely potent anti-inflammatory, antifungal, antifungal antibacterial and antifungal agent. It is a natural treatment for digestive disease, mood ailments, viruses such as herpes and shingles, and feelings of despair, depression, and despair. Even though most men and women place this luscious herb from the garden for its aromatic odor, they soon find the effects in their disposition to be uplifting and transformative. Recent research has indicated that the herb's antioxidant and polyphenol profile enhance memory, enhances focus and clarity, and could have the ability to fight Alzheimer's disease and cell regeneration. Lemon balm was utilized throughout the Middle Ages throughout Europe from Greeks and Romans for all from grooming sword wounds to turning baldness to healing fainting.

Thought to be "an elixir of life" at a stage, physicians were not too far away, given what is known today by scientists.

4.68 Peppermint

Peppermint was known as a "burst of pure Green energy" It is not that there are not more potent stimulants, but not one makes You feel renewed and refreshed. It is useful for curing nausea, relieving stomach discomfort, and draining the mouth of filthy tastes. Its bright, fresh flavor is a Frequent ingredient in Eat the refreshing herb or prepared as an extract for slow digestion. Refreshing mouthwash. Due to its sweet, refreshing taste, peppermint is Frequently utilized in formulations to help cover the taste of less yummy herbs. Even though Peppermint dries nicely, it's yummy when freshly harvested in your garden.

Conclusion

This publication is directed at anyone who wishes to learn about these herbal medicines. I aimed first to make sure you know the idea herbal medicine, herbal medication spade, five needs to herbs, treatments with herbal medicine for hair, face, psychological wellness and a few different kinds of ailments.

Today, over three-quarters of this world uses herbal medication. Western scientists have demonstrated in research that generations have passed down for many years: Plants developed and utilized at home are good at treating non-life-threatening ailments, and injuries or disorders such as lumps, bruises, headaches, fever, anxiety, depression, tiredness, and much more. As you completed the book, I wish you the very best of luck and invite you to love yourself as you proceed, handling the articles ready for you personally and to apply what you have learned to herbal medicine. Herbalism is the medication of those: It is not rocket science. There are loads of scientific and detailed avenues to explore up to your fascination --and program --permits. But fundamentally, herbalism is a cheap, accessible means to look after your health. It may be useful to consider many herbs, such as vegetables. One motive herbalism could be so successful as preventative and curative medicine is since, in many situations, the herbs we utilize today as medication are plants that were considered "vegetables" through all human history. So often today, the kinds of disorders we see are because of a deficiency of essential nutrients. On the most elementary level, herbs may help us fill in such gaps and maintain our bodies moving strong. This analogy applies to how we take our herbaceous plants, too: If herbs are similar to vegetables, then one capsule of herbaceous plants is most likely not likely to be sufficient! Indeed, some herbaceous plants should be taken in tiny doses. However, most herbs we utilize need to be dosed longer about "serving size" than how our culture generally believes about "medicine.".

Good Luck!

The Healing Power of Essential Oils

Soothe Inflammation, Boost Mood, Prevent Autoimmunity, and Feel Great in Every Way

INTRODUCTION

Since ancient times essential oil has been available, and early Egyptians were given credits when essential oils were used for cosmetics, perfumes, and embalming purposes. For example, sandalwood, peppermint, lavender oil, citronella oil, and eucalyptus are essential oils, etc. The essential oil is named from the plant material in which it was extracted, depend on the given an example.

Primary oils are produced in various ways. Most of these are made through distillation (steam distillation). Distillation is a mechanism by which liquids with different vapor pressures are separated. In chemistry, we have learned that the higher vapor pressure substance has a lower boiling point. This process is illustrated in the next paragraph. The plant material is therefore kept in a pressing material or stored in a particular container where liquids can evaporate. Liquid substances are first distilled in plants with low boiling points, while liquid material with higher boiling points remains as in essential oils. However, other essences (essential oils) are so difficult to extract that they have to undergo a complex process. Examples are jasmine and rose oils. They undergo a strict distillation process by first washing a mixture of process-derived essential oils into a sea of osmotic material (supercritical hexane or carbon dioxide). The concrete must then be subjected, using alcohol-based materials, to a second stage in the distillation process and effectively insulate various volatile (absolute) oil from the distilled contents.

Because of their molecular structure, essential oils can penetrate our skin. These molecules are so small that they move seamlessly through our skin. Not all of the essential oil will get into your bloodstream and evaporate as soon as it reaches our skin. Since carrying oils have a large molecular structure, some of the essential oils remain mixed with carrier oil on top of your skin. This offers you more benefits. Not only can you get the essential oils that penetrate the skin, but your skin's oil has many medicinal advantages as well.

CHAPTER ONE
Essential Oil Therapy

Herbs grown on land are known to have some biological activities, which are strongly opposed to contemporary medicines. This is due in particular to the calming effects since most of these natural herbs have gradual healing properties and release the patient from the least side effects. However, this doesn't give grown herbs a rim over those cultivated in the sea. Like herbs grown on land, it is also worth noting that those raised in the sea have therapeutic components. In fact, every natural herb should be seen as having something unique that helps people greatly. Indispensable curative oils can be extricated from these plants. The Reed Essential Oil from the natural yet common plant is a good example. The value of this oil can be understood only if its use is underlined.

The plant in reed is typically widespread in Africa and measures 2.9 mm by 1-1 m. It buds from later summer stages and is popular in the wetlands. The plant is used for several purposes. It's a food-producing crop. Headache and convulsion are also remedied by oil or juice derived from it. The stalks could also be used to tackle mats and containers. Given the medicinal value of the plant, it is questioned why the plant was never developed.

The reed plant has always been in nature. A close look at the Chinese natural medicine chest would imply that the Chinese knew about this plant more than a thousand years ago. Remember that Chinese people are highly celebrated in natural medicine for their knowledge and love. This is known in China as Lu Gen and is widely used in the treatment of fever, cough, and other body conditions. The roots are nutritious and edible due to their rich properties in sugar and starch. In fact, the whole plant is considered to be beneficial to humans. The material of the reed plant is ideal as a medicinal plant. The roots are known to act like medication for cough, brain stimulants and are used to regulate blood sugar levels and to decrease body temperature.

The plant has incredible healing abilities. It is used as an anti-inflammatory to annoyances in the lungs and stomach; it catalysis the release of juice in the body to calm down thirst; it serves as a solution to food poisoning, and it mysteriously breaks up gall stone in the body. There are so many medicinal qualities of the reed plant that only the plant can be experienced.

The shoulder plant can grow in any wet environment. While the man did not investigate the value of this plant, it is still one of man's most valuable herbs, and it is thankful for its healing powers.

The Impact Of Essential Oils On The Body

Some people think that the only real benefit of essential oils is a good fragrance, but in reality, these scents can be powerful. Why not try splattering a few drops of essential oil on your skin when you like to smell amazing and think about the effect the chemical scent has on your body. This helps you to give your well-being a real boost. Check out how these naturally occurring compounds can actually be therapeutic.

Almost every essential oil is, to some extent, antiseptic. Anti-bacterial, anti-fungal, anti-virus, and anti-microbial properties are well known to occur in oils like citrus, tea tree, thyme, eucalyptus, lavender, pine. Using these scents on your body can actually improve your health, rather than cause skin irritation when you wear synthetic fragrances.

A variety of oils may be used to relieve inflammation. Red and swollen tissue can cause much pain and discomfort. Rose, camomile, lavender, myrrh, and sandalwood are the oils that have anti-inflammatory effects.

Cell regeneration and tissue function restoration can occur if a compound has a cytophylactic property. Certain essential oils have this potential. For example, basil, pine, and rosemary can help restore adrenal gland function, while jasmine, ylang, and cypress can improve endocrine glands, with the supposedly aiding regeneration of skin cells by camomile and lavender.

Certain oils have a sedative effect on the nervous system, ideal for muscle spasms and related pain. Plant extracts of this capacity include neroli, lavender, ylang, rose, and geranium. Even when used sparingly, these oils can have a significant effect.

For many years, essential oils have been used to encourage health and well-being. While we now prefer to focus on modern approaches to the treatment of ill-health and illness, we should not neglect the importance of using this natural approach. The healing strength of the fragrances of plants is genuine.

Try choosing an all-natural option when you next buy a perfume. Besides the fantastic smell, you can also improve your fitness. Why spend money on artificial fragrances if there are so many healthy and desirable natural fragrance oils. Find out in detail about this topic, and the power of these compounds will surprise you.

Advantages of Essential Oils and Aromatherapy

The benefits of essential oils are obvious from plants and have life-enhancing functional benefits. These oils are a byproduct of the metabolism of the plant and are known to be its immune system. They are obtained from several component of the plant as stems, petals, seeds, bark, leaves and roots or from citrus peels by steam distillation, which is the purest method of doing so.

Contrary to the word that defines them, these oils don't have an oily look. Most are apparent, perhaps, some of them are diluted to the apricot kernel, sweet almond, or grape seed with a carrier oil.

What are its Essential Oils and Aromatherapy?

The use of pure essential oils to enable physical and mental health is aromatherapy. It is a method of disseminating pure essential oils that is then absorbed into the skin and inhaled. Smell has a strong effect on how we react to our environment physically, emotionally, and mentally.

Many scents every day remind us of the various seasons, a place or circumstance, and happier times. This can also affect our physical, mental, and emotional health. Essential oils. The inhalation of these oils can also affect the release of brain chemical products like serotonin.

How is it used?

Every oil is unique with different methods of application. It can be used in an electrical or candle-type diffuser, mixed with water for use on your skin as a mist, mixed in bottle oil, or applied to soap, lotion, and other body care items.

The aid of bergamot, geraniums, and lavender can be found for tension, depression, and fatigue. Eucalyptus stimulates a strong antiseptic and antihistamine, along with oregano. Orange neroli is ideal for insomnia, and rosemary is an ideal stimulant both for the body and the mind, as well as for rest at the end of a long day.

How long are they working?

After absorption or inhalation by the skin, they exhale and sweat the body in about four hours effectively. Thus, there is no residual accumulation or side effects frequently associated with pharmaceuticals.

How to store essential oils?

In their storage, caution must be exercised. Keep them away from exposure to extreme temperature or heat changes in dark, airproof, glass bottles. Be very respectful and responsible since these are concentrated oils. Keep them out of children's reach.

Organic or non-organic

Natural oils are distilled or extracted from non-pesticidal, herbicide, irradiation, or some other form of unnatural treatment in plants. Non-organic oils can contain substances that are harmful and unnatural and may cause harm or allergy to allergies. You can pay more for organic oils due to the higher cost of organic processing.

Purchase or make your own essential oils

It is vital to check the information supplied to their products by the merchants. In the end, the decision is yours, and you can find the mix that best suits your needs based on your research.

Significant oils may also be purchased as mixtures. But when you don't mix it yourself, there is no control over the mixture. The key benefits of making your own are the savings created from not personally purchasing all essential oil. However, your own mixing can be a problem consistently.

Important advice on oil purchases

Do not buy something in a clear glass bottle as light can destroy properties; do not buy something in plastic that can contaminate; do nothing in a rubber dropper that can melt and contaminate. Finally, search for a supplier who is testing oils and selling samples.

How to Mix and Match Essential Oils

A variety of uses for essential oils, including aromatherapy and many other items, are available in the entire home; you can apply them to the pool, steam inhalation, cold and hot compresses, blend them into face creams, body lotions, use them in the treatment of hair as fragrances in the room or personal perfumes and more.

They are very concentrated and potent (rarely used without dilution and in very particular cases) and are heavily diluted before use. Many are light, clear, although some are vicious and some colorful. They are also extremely volatile and easily evaporated when exposed to air and are best stored in bottles of airtight dark glass. You can dissolve them in fatty oils, including almond, sunflower oil, or alcohol, though. For example, in massage oil, the dilution of essential oil in the base oil is about 2 or 3 percent.

They evaporate as soon as they are in contact with the air, and a certain amount is still inhaled, regardless of the method of application. Since body massage is the primary method of application, the lungs and skin play a primary role in the way they get into the body and function.

There are many ways to use essential oils at home, with or without the aromatherapist's unique guidance and help. As long as you obey the directions and instructions, it can be both enjoyable and satisfying to use them at home. If physical distress is to be handled, you primarily concentrate on its physical properties. You can, for example, choose a person who can battle bacterial infection, such as benzoin, lavender, thyme, or rosewood if you have a sore throat. They have been selected on other occasions for more cosmetic, sedative, stimulant or antidepressant, and elevating skincare properties. A brief holistic analysis of the way essential oils influences you as a whole is often given, but this is not always the key consideration.

Many essential oil applications are possible, such as mixing into your bath water, massage, skin, and hair care or simply for relaxation. You will benefit from the essential oils by selecting the right mixtures.

Essential Oils for Health and Healing

The offer of essential oils by Itself, the real force of its possibilities, is much greater than the sense of smell. A crucial fluid (essential oil) from bulbs, shrubs, leaves, plants, roots, and seeds is distilled. This fluid in the plant plays a significant role in its own biological function and is, therefore, "important" to the life of plants. An example of this is that the essential oil (oils) in a plant's leaf attracts pollinating insects and repels the pests, bacteria, and viruses which threaten their life. The plant's oil has the vibrational capacity to maintain the very survival of the plants.

The same energy will enter the cells of the human body and heal on the fundamental, physical level of the human body if removed (distilled). Whether given to the skin or the air, the oil molecules are used as a healing tool. (Some oils are too heavy to be added directly to the skin; however, they can be diluted with high-grade oil).

Essential oils are used in alternative aromatherapy treatment practices. Aromatherapy is a particular branch of herbal medicine, which uses the healing properties of different plant oils. The history of essential oils goes back more than 120 years as a Europe-wide healing method. Today in France, there is a method of medicinal aromatherapy.

The physiological implications of the scent of the oil are caused by the limbic system. The limbic system is directly linked to brain sections that regulate heart rate, respiration, blood pressure, stress levels, memory, and hormonal balance.

Scientists have learned that inhaling essential oil fragrances is one of the greatest ways to accomplish physiological and psychological impacts. Leading aromatherapy researchers in England have found that oils like jasmine, orange, and rose have a calming effect. These oils transform the brain wave into a rhythm that induces tranquility and well-being. The energy response is improved by stimulating oils – black pepper, basil, cardamom, and rosemary.

Essential oils can be used to treat conditions from skin disorders and infections through to immune and stress deficiencies. The oils have no severe and deadly side effects. The outcomes of genuine healing will differ based on family background, lifestyle, and diet. Unlike prescription medications, the essential oils function in harmony and equilibrium with the body.

Some oils, among others, are potent antimicrobial agents without the harmful side effects of traditional antibiotics. Cinnamon and eucalyptol oils have the same power as traditional antibiotics against certain microorganisms and are particularly effective against influenza viruses. The typical treatment for sore throats and laryngitis was sandalwood oil. Lavender oil has a drastic cure for burns. The antimicrobial effects of oils are due to their capacity to penetrate microbial cell walls and to cut off oxygen. This prevents energy formation in microbial cells and destroys them.

Safeguards must be taken while using essential oils. Some oils can cause an internal toxic reaction. Their toxicity is, therefore, much lower when externally applied. Such high-phenol (disinfectant) oils should not be taken internally for a prolonged period (over 10-21 days), as this can have an effect on some aspects of liver metabolism.

CHAPTER TWO
Essential Oils and Soul-Level Healing

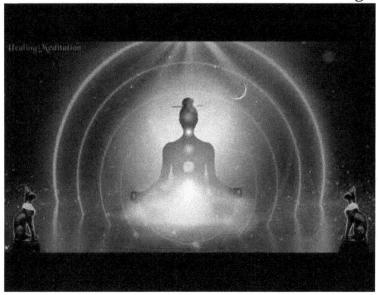

The plant's spirit carries essential oils. "Matter is most sacred in the fragrance of the plant .... When the spirit approaches the real world more closely, we have an appreciation of fragrance."

The soul of man includes components of plants, animals, and human souls. Every one of us, therefore, has the capacity to bind plant souls on a soul-to-soul basis. When the human soul is concerned with life's everyday problems, reasonable consciousness becomes disconnected from the higher self and attached to the "stubbornness."

The plant soul is not burdened with vanity; thus, it has the virtues of pureness and infinity. Therefore, if provided to the human soul, the individualized plant soul combination in a core oil mix is able to be received with excitement and impulse the latter to step beyond restriction by shifting its orientation from the finite to the infinite.

The secret to this is the formulation of an oil blend that accurately represents a person's true self. Living in the true nature of the soul requires a continuous link to the higher self. The secret to well-being is bliss. No disappointed person can be very good. The secret to happiness, however, is that we embrace and act according to our authentic selves and understand others. To heal with essential oils on the soul level, you need to know the inner or soul essence of any essential oil.

Using creative awareness

In this discussion, the term creative consciousness refers to overcoming the limitations of the study by senses and intellect of the material aspects of essential oils through a complementary understanding of the spiritual roots, which help these material aspects. The plant soul, like the human soul, comprises the metaphysical origins of the material and bioenergy manifestations of plants. Thus all the biophysical and bioenergy characteristics of the plant are used to establish an understanding of spiritual roots when using essential oils for the spiritual work of the soul.

Plants are alive, and any living thing is enshrouded. Just like every soul of us is unique and has specific individual characteristics and tangible attributes, so are planting souls. The unique mix of archetypal attributes that are encrypted in each soul gives rise to different traits and behavioral styles in our lives.

Similarly, biochemistry, shape, growth characteristics, therapeutic characteristics, and historical and folk associations of a plant are representations or pictures of the archetypal attribute's constituent by their spirit. These archetypal images can be used to describe the unique essence of the true selves of an essential oil-its natural manifestation.

If essential oils are merged together with a sense of the real inner character of each oil, the oils in the mixture combine and form a unique, structured, soil-powered substance that is stronger than the sum of its elements. When diverse soul energies are thus aligned, the integrated soul intensity reveals what is called evolving behavior. This, in turn, can be used to catalyze evolving practices in the human soul aimed at harmonization and cultivating the true self of the human being.

In early childhood, we usually forsake ourselves when we are taught that they are not enough. We trade our natural speech for a survival personality that, works and meets the endorsement of our parents, teachers, etc. In the end, we are separated from the true self, the 'living soul,' and this separation fuel the sense of the incompleteness, solitude, and discord which we seek for all our lives.

The secret to soul reintegration through essential oil work is the ability to look beyond its biochemistry and therapeutic acts and to recognize the unique soul essence of each fuel oil, the metaphysical source of the physical properties of the fuel oil. When this is completed, the plant souls in oils will reciprocate, and the soul encounter between the human soul and plant will be illumined by the spirit.

The more essential oils you are able to understand at this stage, the greater the complex potential of making combinations that influence the soul more profound and deeper and enlighten it, from the inertial stubbornness and fragmentation to the entire soul-to-soul relationship with all elements of the natural world. This helps you to re-establish the natural capacity to bind earthly fire with heavenly light, lost in early childhood.

Natural Herpes Cure With Essential Oils

While herpes is not cured, there are several natural ways of suppressing and treating herpes symptoms (oral and genital). They explain how to combine different herbs, make balsamic and ingest oils, or put essential oils on your skin in every work written in these natural treatments. The problem with these treatments is the preparation, from the procurement of ingredients to the preparation and implementation of them in a particular way. When you buy some essential oil, you can't go to any store just to find essential oil that is safe to eat or put on your skin, and who will tell you how to use it safely and effectively? When you feel run down, wounded, sorry, and/or ashamed about being seen with cold wrath, you won't go shopping and make the arrangements to feel better together; you want something that you can do for yourself. It is not difficult to find all-natural treatments for oral and genital herpes. The hard part is to understand what is there, why it works, and how it's safe to use.

You should look for a company that tells you of the elements in the product and guarantees its promises of efficacy when purchasing a product to fight the symptoms and outbreaks of herpes.

The main ingredients in many natural herpes treatments are essential oils. When purchasing and using essential oil products, you should know carefully what a therapeutic oil (grade A) is and is like in a non-graded essential oil. A grade-A therapeutically oil means the percentages determined in a gas chromatography profile are kept up to the level of minimum and maximum chemical components. Simply specifying that each essential oil has key chemicals that make up the oil, and these constituents must be considered a therapeutic grade oil (grade A) in a certain percentage (min. to the max.). If it did not fall in these parameters, chemistry (non-therapeutic) would be considered lower.

They are standards of purity and dignity in Europe set by the French Normalization Organization Regulation (AFNOR). These principles are not used in the United States. Any US bottle of oil will claim 100% pure and average and not entirely therapeutic. That means the US requires no grading because what you place on your skin (which is ingestion) can not be guaranteed to be pure or therapeutic. Any critical oil companies in the United States only adopt these requirements because they decide to have a superior product. Any oil can be broken up, which means that some of the ingredients are lacking and can not become medicinal; in reality, it can intensify the condition. You will never tell whether the oil is fragmented by the scent except with a very well-trained nose. A Grade A medicinal oil is the only way to ensure that you can buy from a business that guarantees it. If it matters to the company, it's worth buying from you the best.

Essential Oils Power

Some essential oils have the ability to break the cell membrane of the herpes virus, and the virus can not survive without this membrane. After the membrane is removed, the virus has no control and can start healing instantly. Even though many essential oils have this ability, it is extremely necessary to use oil, for example, oregano oil, which will dismantle and kill the virus before oregano burns the skin. You don't want to kill the virus and then face skin burning, thick scabbing, and healing. This is why the remainder of the healing process must also be taken into consideration while using a product. Ensure that a commodity addresses all healing phases.

-- Destroy the virus

-- Eliminate pain

-- Reduction of inflammation

-- Skin mitigation

Powerful Health Benefits of Essential Oils

An aromatic liquid is an essential oil that is distilled in different parts of the plant. They are very concentrated with the true essence of the plant and 75 to 100 times more influential than herbs.

The essential oil is intended to keep the plant functional. This is done by guarding the plant against insects and other herbicides, fungi, bacteria, and micro-organisms. They also enable plants to cure injuries. These qualities make it very beneficial for the human race.

Essential oils can affect the mind as well as the body. Their capacity to influence people at all levels is an unmatched element of other healing arts.

There are three ways to receive the health advantages of essential oils. They can be used topically by directly applying them to the skin. Some oils are caustic and may require dilution. They can be used diffused or internally. Never use essential oils in the ears or eyes as these layers are very fragile. Whether the oil is absorbed, inhaled, or taken by the skin, it works therapeutically once it is in the bloodstream, regardless of how low a dose.

Here are ways to use essential oils for your everyday health advantages for you and your family:

Increase your stamina and memory: Drink a glass of water with 2-3 drops of essential lemon, orange, or peppermint oil.

Immune boost: Add oregano, frankincense thyme on the bottom of your feet after a shower. (3 to 4 drops)

Protect against bacteria, fungus, and microbes: Use the blend to protect the diffuser from microbes in your home or workplace.

Eradicate stomach upset: In warm water, take one or two drops of cinnamon bark oil and drink as a tea.

Stop headaches: Massage the temples with lavender oil, head, and forehead; lie down for 10 minutes and inhale the oil deeply on your palms.

Protect motion sickness: Sprinkle a few drops of peppermint oil or ginger on the tissue and allow your sick child to inhale it while driving on a vehicle.

Study aid: Experiment with the diffusion of one of those essential oils near the area of study to enhance concentration and concentration: grapefruit, lemon, bergamot, peppermint, or pine.

Insomnia: Put two drops of lavender oil on a tissue and tuck it below the pillow.

Heal canker sores: Put myrrh on the canker sore to heal quickly.

Cold and cough: Massage the immune system is a combination of the back, chest, and foot.

Essential oils are not fatty but soothing and soft. They are the best way to fix problems caused by inadequate nutrition, chemicals, and stress.

The protection and life changes in essential oils are entirely dependent on their pureness and consistency. In general, the essential oil found in department stores and even health food stores is of unknown consistency and not suitable to be consumed or cured. Only essential and pure oil can be used for the best performance.

Experience and find your essential oils, which make a real change in your life. Aromatherapy's entire premise is that it should be a fun experience. There should be more than one oil you can use for a specific condition, so you can find one you prefer.

Essential Oils Used in Aromatherapy to Treat Anxiety

There are many natural solutions to anxiety, such as the St. John's Word and Passion Flower, which can maintain a relaxed mood while elevating the spirits. Reducing stress will be beneficial in reducing anxiety naturally. Yoga, meditation, music, relaxation, a good book all contributes to stress reduction.

The essential oils used in aromatherapy to treat anxiety are a wonderful complement to yoga and meditation. The following list of essential oils for treating anxiety and depression in aromatherapy is given;

A fresh, spicy, sweet, licorice-like scent of anise (Pimpinella anisum). Anise seed has been used as a spice and medicine for many years. The seed is flavored with Raki, a popular drink in Turkey. Health conditions like asthma, bronchitis, headache, indigestion, cramps, bloating, coughs, bug bites, stress, nausea, and digestion are beneficial to anise. It combines well with bay, black pepper, orange, ginger, lavender, pine, and rose in aromatherapy. Do not mix Anise seed oil (Pimpinella anisum) with Illicium vernum (Anise Star oil) derived from the tree fruit. Anise seed oil will crystallize due to the anethole content in the oil at cool temperatures. Stop in epilepsy, even when breast-feeding or pregnant. May cause irritation of the skin.

The fresh, spicy, warm, and herbaceous flavor of Basil (Ocimum basilicum). Basil is a holy plant used in ayurvedic medicine in India. It was used as a strewing herb for scent reduction and had many culinary applications. Basil is added to abrasions, bronchitis, anxiety, cough, colds, depression, flatulence, exhaustion, exhaustion, infection, bug bites and repellents, sinuses, cough whips. Basil can be added to a hair tonic to boost growth. Bergamot, citrus oils, citronella, geranium, clary sage, opopanax, hyssop, and rosemary mix well. Stop epilepsy, liver, and fertility issues. It can cause irritation of the skin.

Citrus aurantium (Bergamot) has a fresh, herbal, floral, citrus smell. In Italian folk culture, Bergamot was used as a cure for fever and had a long history in potpourri and perfumes. It is advantageous for abscesses, anxiety, acne, boils, bronchitis, carbuncles, colds, colds, colic, cystitis, eczema, depression, fever, halitosis, herpes, flatulence, insect dents, parasites, nervous tensions, oily teint, psoriasis, respiratory tract, throat sore, varicose veins. Fill in the bergamot with a massage mixture for indigestion. Rub the abdomen clockwise. Bergamot is commonly thought to be healthy and well blended with citrus oils, chamomile, coriander, cypress, geranium, helichrysum, jasmine, juniper, lavender, lemon ball, nutmeg, neroli, rose, sandalwood, vetiver, purple, ylang, and vetiver.

The woody, balsamic scent of the Cedarwood atlas with its rich dry overtones. Oil was traditionally used for the infection of the bronchial and urinary tract. Cedarwood also has a long tradition of perfume and incense. The wood was burnt to the air by the Greeks and the Romans. Cedarwood benefits acne, cleaning of the air, anxiety, arthritis, bronchitis, bronchitis, cough, dandruff, dry skin, fungus, immune stimulants, insecticide, nerve tension, rheumatism, rashes, ulcers. Cedarwood is a good addition to a hair tonic and gives a lasting undertone to the aroma. Bergamot, chamomile, clary wise, eucalyptus, cypress, jasmine, lavender, juniper, neroli, palmarosa, petty grain, vetiver, sandalwood, ylang-ylang mixes well. Stop using during pregnancy. It can cause irritation of the skin.

The fresh, woody, spicy, bauxitic aroma of Frankincense (Boswellia carterii) has top-notch citrus. Frankincense's everyday use has a long history as incense. The Egyptians have burned it, and it is used in many religious ceremonies. It was traditionally used for skin disorders from acne to wound healing. Incense benefits anxiety, acne, blemishes, asthma, bronchitis, coughs, colds, dry skin, flu, nervousness, rheumatism, skin pain, stress, sores, wrinkles, urinary tract infections, wounds. Skin suppressions. To use any of the skin healing properties of this oil, skin creams or toners may be applied. Combine well with bergamot, black pepper, pepper, cinnamon, geranium, grapefruit, lavender, citrus fruit, neroli, orange, mandarin, palmarosa, patchouli, pine, Rose, grapefruit, vetiver, ylang-ylang. Frankincense has many other names, such as Frankincense. You most often see it as frankincense, oliban, or Boswellia, and it is considered safe in general.

The new, tangy citrus scent and common use of grapefruit (Citrus paradisi) are olive oil, used by the fragrance industry and used as a stimulant and antidepressant in medicine. It also helps acne, anxiety, cellulite, chills, colds, depression, nausea, gall bladder, headache, headaches, jet lags, tiredness of muscle, weakness of the nerve, obesity, oily skin and hair, poor circulation, stealth, stress, skin and tissue tones, water retention. This oil may be spread into the air or added to a salve that can be applied to the temples and neck to aid in tiredness, tension, and exhaust—well, Mixed With bergamot, dark pepper, cardamom, sage clary, clove, cypress, eucalyptus, fennel, candy, fog, geranium, ginger, jumper, lavender, citrus fruit, mandarin, neroli, palm pigs, patchouli, peppermint, rosemary, thyme, ylang. Stop during your pregnancy. Phototoxic. Phototoxic.

Jasmine has a soft, rich, and profoundly floral fragrance. Jasmine is a perfumery product with a long history, like Cleopatra and Louis XVI. It is also used for headaches and skin problems. Benefits: spasms, cough, depression, dysmenorrhea, eczema, headache, labor pains, laryngitis, stimulus memory, menstrual issues, prostate issues, skin irritation, tension. Try adding Jasmine to a mixture to use when you research and see if it helps with your memory. Well, Blends with Bergamot, clary wise, clove, clove, ginger, grapefruit, lemon, mandarin, neroli, orange, palmarosa, petty-grain, rose, sandalwood, ylang handling. The processing of 1 lb. of oil requires around 2,000 lbs. of jasmine flowers. This oil is darkened by age. Stop breastfeeding or pregnancy. It can cause irritation of the skin. Not to be used internally.

Marjoram has a luminous and sweet balsamic taste and is used as both a culinary and medicinal herb. It is a lovely herb since it soothes digestive, respiratory, and nervous diseases. Amenorrhea, anxiety, bronchitis, hypertension, insomnia, coldness, constipation, cough, dysmenorrhea, flatulence, headache, insomnia, leucorrhea, ailments and stiffness, strains, sore throats, vertigo. Add marjoram to a massage oil mix for muscle aches and pains and as a soothing agent. Mix well with basil, bergamot, dark pepper, cedarwood, camomile, cypress, eucalyptus, eucalyptus lemon, fennel, lavender, citrus fruit, orange, peppermint, pine, rosemary, tea-tree, thyme. The Greeks called this plant a mountain joy and treated it as a sign of happiness. Stop during your pregnancy.

The Citrus aurantium (Neroli or Orange Blossom) is a soft, sweet floral fragrance with a terpenic top notch. In perfumery neroli, the base note, as well as the top note, depends on the oils with which it is mixed. It is also renowned for its relaxing effects. Benefits: anxiety, cold, colic, depression, flatulence, flu, general skincare, headache, insomnia, oily and dry skin, poor blood circulation, skin scars, fragile skin, shock, sluggish digestion. This oil's sedative properties make it a pleasant addition to a bath for all ages. Well, blends with benzoin, chamomile, sage, coryan, candy, geranium, ginger, jasmine, grapefruit, lavender, juniper, lemon, myrrh, mandarin, orange, palmarosa, petitgrain, sandalwood, rose, ylang, andlang. ylang. It takes about 100 lbs of flowers to produce 1 lb. of essential neroli oil. Generally deemed secure.

Essential oils are powerful, so never dilute them or take them internally unless you work with a qualified practitioner. Keep essential oils out of infants. After the oil has been dissolved in suitable carrier oil, a small patch test must always be performed on an exposed portion of the body, such as the top of the arm, not on delicate skin.

Using the Magic of Rose Essential Oil

Rose was a lasting sign of love and beauty in history. The flora is very complex, with deep hues, luxurious petals, and an absolutely magnificent flavor. The same beauty is found in the rose flowers' aromatic oils. Not only is the smell sweet, rich, and distinguishing, but rose oil is used today for the most diverse healing applications of any essential oil. The oil is considered a supreme body and soul healer and can be used effectively with simple natural healing technologies.

Rose essential oil is becoming more and more popular, which is interesting now that its unique healing applications are most needed around the world. Real Rose oils are the first choice to open the heart chakra, an opening which many people strive to inspire; this heart-opening action bears witness to the valid symbol of love. The rose essential oil, which also shows its ability to boost the appearance, is a crucial ingredient in the finest skincare products. It's also a powerful antiviral and antidepressant, all of this in a small bottle concentrated. What makes rose oil so unique, and how can anyone (not just enthusiasts of natural health) use its plentiful healing activities?

Rose essential oil is an excellent liquid. It really is a great concentration of rose flowers: only a few drops of rose are required. The yield of rose oil is, on average, one kilogram per 2,500 kilos Roses under the most favorable conditions. This quantity of roses might take more than four times to make the same quantity of oil if the weather was less than favorable. Think about it — it's difficult to imagine how 2,500 kilograms (more than 5,000 pounds) of roses look! And the oil itself is naturally a combination of more than 300 individual molecules, all of which need to be defined through scientific methods. It is this beautiful mixture of deep focus and alchemy of Mother Nature that imparts a fantastic healing value to rose oil.

There are two types of roses: Rose Absolute, both cheaper, is a liquid secure extract. The Absolute odor most like the flora, developed at cool temperatures, leaving most natural components unchanged. The absolute yield is relatively high, so it is a slightly cheaper variety. Rose Otto is this oil distilled in steam, and Rose's real 'essential oil.' While the Absolute retains a deep red flower hue, the Otto has a transparent or slightly pale yellow flavor. Otto's fragrance is brilliant and uplifting with bright, sweet notes. Bulgaria is the most well-known rose-growing country and produces the most common differences of each oil type. Rose Otto is also manufactured in Turkey in large amounts, while the Absolute is also widely manufactured in Morocco.

When looking at the medicinal uses of oils, we must take the whole intellectual body/complex into consideration — instead of divorcing the two too frequently done in western medicine. Rose essential oil is very physiologically active, but it is when the emotions and spirits are approached that Rose truly shines. Otto is an effective antiviral used by many people to treat herpes and shingles. Given its power, it is still soft enough to be used undilutedly on the skin. Rose oils are also deeply useful tonics for the reproductive system of women; they are said to improve fertility and cause uterus and ovary health. For these reasons, a dilute formula of 3% Rose oil may be regularly massaged in the lower abdomen.

The most popular medicinal application can be used in many of the finest cosmetics in the world for skincare. Rose extracts are used. Rose Otto can minimize inflammation, cure capillaries, moisture and fatigue and serve as an efficient astringent and antiseptic. The 1% concentration of any skincare formula will significantly enhance your appearance. Rosewater ('rest' from the distillation process) is excellent preparation for beauty treatment itself. The bath, marketed as 'Rose hydrosol,' is also used as a cleansing tonic on the face with a cotton ball.

While not the most popular, Rose's most effective therapeutic application as a healer of the Soul is undoubted. The aromas of the Absolute, as well as the Otto, are popular antidepressants, an activity not clearly described by modern medicine. The olfactory sense is one of those five senses that are directly connected to the brain and has a profound root in our overall well-being. For this reason, Rose Absolute can be frayed as a natural perfume, often diluted in jojoba oil to 10% and tangled in the wrists and throat. The Otto will do the same, but it could be even more helpful and smaller than aromatherapy massage oil. Rose's inhalation and topical treatment were thought to regulate the movement of Chi into the liver in esoteric medicines. This is of great function because it is a blocked flow of this Chi, which can cause frustration, discomfort, and anxiety. Perhaps the most significant influence is that we strengthen the heart chakra so that we are more responsive, caring, receptive, and relaxed to one another in times of stress.

It is enjoyable and convenient to use the soothing properties of rose oils. Absolute and Otto are safe and can be used without dilution wherever you want. Both are considered to be highly potent, but diluting them in carrier oil does not reduce their effectiveness. A 5 to 10% dilution is often used for personal perfume, 1 to 3% for massage oil as well as 1 to 2% for dilution and beauty treatments. Suppose oil can be used alone or combined with other aromatics of your choosing in even the most basic aromatherapy diffusers. There are, of course, other aromatherapy techniques, and you can use your instincts for the right plan.

Rose's essential oils, which seem to be a natural creation of Nature's sign of love and elegance, are considered among the most aromatherapy and transformative. Civilization has acquired the technical know-how to place thousands of Roses in a small bottle and to take them almost instantly around the world. However, Nature created this unique medicine thousands of years ago. If you want a little more beauty and love in your life, try giving essential Rose oils.

CHAPTER THREE
Inflammation

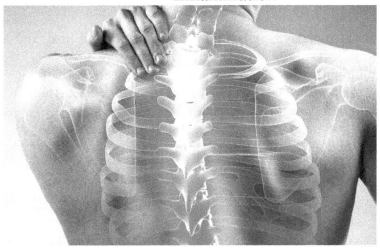

Many people may find it a matter of vanity and indulgence to care for your skin and keep it young and bright, whether via regular facials or quality skincare products. Let's be honest; it's to some extent. We want to look good because we feel better about ourselves when we look good. But it benefits you more than the skin, especially when it comes to inflammation, to appreciating your esthetics.

The skin is your body's largest organ and has many functions that are taken for granted. For example, the bouncer is more than just the bouncer in a nightclub, wrapping your skeletal structure, musculature, and internal organs. It only ensures that the right things come in and keeps some of the most crucial matters out. Like your kidneys, the skin acts as complete waste disposal, and its acidic pH makes this a hostile environment for bacteria to survive.

In the development of skin care, there are many ways to correct aging issues, including hormone balancing, UV protection, free radical damage correction, and detoxification. In recent years, micro-injections have become more popular, and Sirtuin technology has been aimed at activating cell-life enzymes. But what are you aware of inflammation?

We guess what is probably in our mind is redness, swelling, heat, and maybe discomfort. If so, you're on the right track, but we are not talking about inflammation. What's more, you're probably wondering what this has to do with you if you don't have rosacea. What if we tell you about the inflammation, we're talking about is an internal and silent inflammation that you don't see or feel. In other words, if you have inflammation, it doesn't matter if, over the years, you're going to see its effects and the actual impact on your skin (and body in general).

There are two types of aging; you see: extrinsic and intrinsic; it is fairly sure that until now, what you have treated is only irrelevant. As these names suggest, external aging takes place outside the body and is dependent on all the factors that you already know: damaging radiation caused by sun exposure, pollution, and other free radical agents. In contrast, the intrinsic aging takes place inside the body, and genetics and inflammation are the principal factors.

Inflammation is stress-like. It has its advantages when the body works to protect itself. The battle or flight response and the adrenaline spike was an essential tool for the survival of our species. However, chronically elevated adrenaline levels-commonly referred to as stress-break your immune system and made you more susceptible to disease.

Similarly, inflammation is the response of the skin when an unknown element "strikes" the skin. The blood is rushed to the affected zone (increasing heat and skin redness) to help kill the infection in white blood cells. Chronic inflammation (whether or not it is visible) maintains the skin in an increased reaction. When this protective mechanism occurs, enzymes are released, and free radicals are released into cells, including collagen and elastin.

You probably wonder at this point what causes inflammation. It was just said, stress and diet are biggies, although it seems today that stress is the accepted standard in society. And we are not asking you to revise your current lifestyle, it is not only the beauty of your skin but the overall health that changes your diet and the use of the appropriate skin treatment products that makes a significant long-term difference.

Aging is not the only cause of inflammation of the skin over time. Other common problems with the skin include acne, pigmentation, sagging, swollen pores, dryness, sluggishness, skin reddening, and flare-ups.

And how are you coping with this inflammation? I've had consumers too many who feel that the more "fortified" or tougher a substance or procedure, the better. It must mean, after all, that it's more effective, right? Wrong. Wrong.

Believe me, more aggressive procedures may be successful and are required at times, depending on the skin condition and the results to be obtained. Every skin treatment, laser, and skin treatment has its place. These therapies cause injury in the skin, which can help as long as you restore Equilibrium and give your skin the techniques it needs to heal and recover properly from the inside.

Here are some simple measures to start tackling inflammation:

1. Start by adding to your skincare items containing ingredients like allantoin, aloe, ginkgo biloba, honey, and camomile. Skin growth factors (IGFs) are also crucial for skin healing and regeneration.

2. Be sure to wear a sunblock of a broad spectrum on a daily basis, which contains titanium dioxide or zinc oxide in a 6 percent or more active ingredient.

3. Avoid very hot water in your face washing or showers. Instead, use clean water to cool and even hold some skin care products in the fridge for this calming, cooling effect.

4. Include fresh fruit and vegetables with whole grains and salmon in your diet. Omega 3 and 6 supplements of fatty acids are also useful in targeting inflammation when you are not large on fish.

5.Avoid as much sugar and coffee as you can. Black and green tea, besides being full of antioxidants, are perfect caffeine alternatives!

More natural, younger, and radiant skin does not inherently alter your lifestyle entirely, although it needs some adjustments. Operations, botoxes, and fillers will reduce wrinkles, but they do not affect the skin's texture and health. It is not only a superficial fast fix if you want long-term results, but a complete and systematic solution involving the treatment and cure of the skin from the inside out. Who knows, you might even lose your waistline for a few inches!

Treating Inflammation at the Source

Nearly all possible human illnesses or ills, including many inflammatory diseases such as psoriasis or arthritis, have been covered with pulsed electromagnetic fields (PEMFs). PEMF therapy was related to reducing pain and improved healing. The PEMF exercises these effects by controlling, inter alia, biological acts involving autoimmune diseases and inflammation.

What does inflammation mean?

Inflammation is a cascade of physiological processes that are instigated by the body to repair cell damage and restore normal tissue function in tissues that have healthy blood flow.

Inflammation is a net result of a cascade in biological processes that interacts with other cell groups, such as fibroblasts, endothelial, and smooth muscle vascular cells, via the interaction of different immune cell types, including lymphocytes, macrophages, and neutrophils.

Chronic versus Acute inflammation

While inflammation is an essential and vital process, its intensity can be abnormally exacerbated during the initial acute phase and sometimes lasts longer than necessary and develops into chronic inflammation. Chronic inflammation is associated with one or more aspects of the immune system dysfunction and is responsible for persistent harm to the tissues in diseases such as tendonitis, psoriasis or arthritis. Chronic inflammation, among many other disorders, is also a cause of Alzheimer's and cancer disease.

Inflammation mechanics

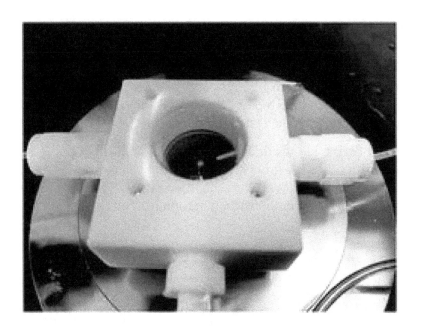

Several types of cell and metabolic pathways that induce inflammation are targeted at various therapies to regulate inflammation in the acute phase and to avoid progression to chronic inflammation. Inflammation can be caused by many causes, and it is necessary to recognize and consider the essence of the cause in the design of therapeutic approaches. In bacterial infections, the arrival of T cells is followed up by early infiltration by polymorphonuclear neutrophils (PMNs), a form of white blood cell, an activity needed to destroy bacteria. In this case, removing T cells can delay or stop healing. T-cells are less critical for repairing tissue damage during trauma-induced injury and can be harmful if present for a long time.

Early removal of T cells in an acute inflammation stage may minimize unnecessary inflammatory effects, speed up treatment, and decrease the risk of chronic inflammatory disease. The survival of the disease state relies on the involvement of T cells in chronic inflammatory diseases such as psoriasis, rheumatoid arthritis, and chronic tendinitis. In this case, the removal of T cells will be a promising therapeutic strategy for these and related chronic conditions. T cells are a major inflammatory cascade regulator. Research has shown that the effects of PEMF on T cell membranes and main enzymes in cells can cause the proper death of T-lymphocytes. PEMFs have, for example, been shown to influence ion flow through specific cell membrane channels, including sodium, potassium, and calcium channels, which influence those enzymes positively. These appropriate effects lead to chronic inflammation reduction.

Cells out of balance and Homeostasis

Normal cells are generally not affected by magnetic fields. Compressed cells are more likely to be damaged, called meta-stable cells. This means that the effect of PEMF is more pronounced in cases of tissue or cell imbalance, i.e., in cases of pathology or chronic inflammation. If homeostasis in the body is robust, it is unlikely that

163

PEMFs, especially low PEMFs, would have an effect. For example, activating the T cell receptor, such as with PPEMF's, often triggers various cell processes that return to normal levels within five minutes of removing the activating signal.

Decreasing of inflammation with PEMF

Other white blood cells are known as the lymphocytes, are greatly affected, both by low intensity, low-frequency PEMF, and also by DC / permanent magnetic fields. PEMF interacts in sometimes unpredictable ways with cell systems. This means that the frequency and duration of the reaction do not always change one-on-one. PEMF inhibits the growth and natural death of unwanted inflammatory lymphocytes. The EMF suppression of lymphocytes and inflammatory procedures 48 and 72 hours after the treatment with EMF is most evident, and its effect on EMF seems to have disappeared. This indicates that the effects of PEMF fit well with other natural therapies.

Inflammatory usage of EMF must be tailored such that exposure leads to long-term therapeutic effects. Higher frequency pulse-burst modulated fields tend to be much more potent than other frequency signals and thus show better therapeutic performance. While some types of signals are most successful, a positive response to different kinds of magnetic stimuli is also seen. Related effects tend to occur on lymphocytes with pulsed bone healing fields versus frequency sinusoidal power line fields. Pulsed PEMFs with 5-25 MilliTesla intensities had no effect on normal T cells. This means that the normal lymphocytes are not apparently damaged.

Interleukin-2 (IL-2) is produced by inflammatory T cells, which stimulates T cell development. When the IL-2 levels are high enough, the desired early removal of chronic inflammatory cells increases, cells exposed to pulsed PEMF can increase IL-2 up to three times. EMF intensity windows appear to exist, but they are not well defined. Frequency windows were found to vary between different tissue cell types in the body. The frequency ranges for bone cells tend to be very narrow. The frequency windows appear to be wider for lymphocytes. Also, 5-100 hertz signals of 0.15 mT modulate the calcium flow of lymphocytes; 50 Hz PEMF is the most successful. Frequency fields were found to have an action in conjunction with parallel static magnetic fields. PEMF affects all lymphocytes, including the B and T cells and other human lymphoid lines.

How and Why You May Have an Autoimmune Disease

An autoimmune disease is a consequence of the immune system's failure or failure. More than 100 immune system disorders exist. Modern medicine cannot describe or establish the causes of autoimmune diseases in particular. Despite advances in technology and science in the field of autoimmunity, dissatisfaction and disappointment remain an essential part of modern medicine.

Autoimmune conditions are becoming more common. Women are usually more vulnerable to them than men. Men have a higher risk of Mellitus and myocarditis than women, and women are three to six times more vulnerable to autoimmune diseases than men. Are you at risk?

It is crucial to know how and why you may have an autoimmune disease.

First and foremost, you must have a layman's term interpretation of the immune system. Your immune system consists of four parts, with each region having its own unique function. The human immune system is extremely complex — a testament to the creativity and mystery of evolution — that it includes not only individual bodies and tissues but the entire human body. The essential purpose of this device is to alert the body about the imminent hazards of bacteria and viruses (sorry, many of us actually miss these narrative signals or fail to decode those messages). Moreover, the immune system "knows" these foreign invaders or antigens (in the future, similar invaders are to be detected for better disease prevention). In addition, the white blood cells in the immune system contain anti kids that are chemicals that bind particular antigens and attack them. These white blood cells send "messages" to prevent "inflammation" from spreading in other areas of the world in response to injury or antigen. In other words, "chemical instructions" are given to cleanse the disease or infection in the bud.

In short, the immune system has various functions to recognize, activate, mobilize, and recover. It understands the future scenario of crime in the city, takes reasonable public safety steps, is educating the local police, and oversees the city's law and order.

Autoimmune happens when the immune system attacks its own cells and confuses them with foreign invaders. It is demonstrated by the autoimmune disease myasthenia gravis as a receptor attack responsible for interactions between the voluntary muscles and the nervous system, leading to a malfunction that results in muscle fatigue, a hallmark feature of myasthenia gravis.

In general, autoimmune disorders have multiple causes.

The onset or worsening of an autoimmune disease can be caused by environmental agents. Mercury, in particular, has a crucial role to play, but the health community has little knowledge about how or why it is to blame for many immune disorders. Studies have shown that Americans who have no direct interaction with heavy metals have over 200 chemicals in their bodies. The number of toxic chemicals present in human beings is so massive and stunning, it goes beyond the handling capacities of the immune system. The scenario can be compared to a police station in a crime-infested town. It usually takes hundreds, if not thousands of years for the immune system to respond to environmental stress. Therefore, the immune system can easily weaken its functions in the very toxic world in which we work, leading to errors and mistakes, which are the root causes of autoimmunity.

The genetic factor is another crucial aspect of the triggers of autoimmune diseases. Unfortunately, you can do nothing with your parents' legacy genes.

Lifestyle and diet can cause an assault as well. For example, insufficient sun vitamin D may be involved in the disease, while too much sun ultraviolet may not help the immune system. A gluten-too-protein diet can cause inflammation in the small intestine, leading to discomfort, and thus block the nutrient absorption. It could induce coeliac disease, which is an autoimmune condition if you are allergic to gluten. The iodine in seafood can be difficult for mice, although it is not found to affect humans.

All in all, not only one factor, but a combination of many factors can cause autoimmune disease. Given the severity of the condition, a holistic approach to the treatment of illness and disorder is essential. Drugs alone are an ineffective solution to autoimmune disorders. Furthermore, drugs can not cure the disease: they at best only aim to suppress those symptoms by weakening the immune system. It is like a police station where some bad guys are inside the police department. You basically disarm all the police without knowing the wrong guys to prevent the wrong guys from causing trouble. As wise, the use of drugs to suppress an "overactive" immune system reduces some of the symptoms but also weakens the immune system.

Homeopathy Treatment for an Autoimmune Skin Disorder

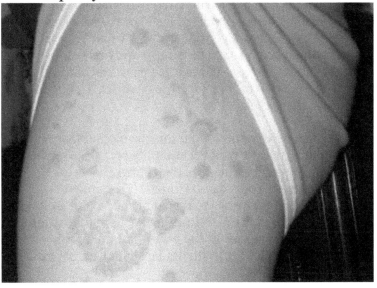

The chronic "psoriasis" skin condition causes patients to suffer from red and skin formations. Joints are also affected, and patients feel anxious when their limbs are moving. Like other skin issues, it is not infectious. Psoriasis breaks out in patches after inflamed by excess cell production, which is medically referred to as psoriatic plaques. These patches appear white and accumulate with productive excess skin.

167

They are often seen in the joints-knees and elbows. There are several claims that patients suffer from these patches on their scalp.

Simply stated, it is chronic, and the severity varies from patient to patient. Worldwide, skin specialists claim patients with small patches and patients with full patches have been seen all over the body. In some cases, joint dolor is also reported, particularly in severe cases. It is not possible to speak about the exact cause of this disorder. It is in the genes of the person that makes him/her suffer from psoriasis. So far, no exact cause has been identified; doctors claim it is hereditary. It is an autoimmune disease of the skin.

How does it cause, and what happens?

Genes are an essential factor in this disorder. If the immune system of a person may block viral infection, the cause of the condition is not available. Here is the necessary knowledge about "the effects of the immune system and the causes of psoriasis." Medically, physicians or specialists describe this as damage to the T lymphocyte, one of three white blood cell types. The development of the skin cells is usually incremental. Fresh cells will take over the old ones when they shed; this doesn't happen much because old cells flake away after four weeks. When talking about the non-contagious psoriasis of the skin condition, it alters the process of replacing the old cells. The period is limited to days rather than weeks.

Different patients of age group suffer from this problem. Most patients are in adulthood, whilst puberty and puberty take a small percentage. On the body sections, such as the elbows, knees, scalp, and back, plaques and dense spots can be found. It becomes humiliating for a patient when he has to reveal his body. For example, adolescents with psoriasis will avoid swimming because they would display the patches created because of the non-inflammatory health issue. Similarly, in their regular life, patients face many embarrassing scenarios.

What are the available signs and treatments?

The cause of psoriasis may be identified with various symptoms. In moderate cases, small parts of the skin are rash, and in extreme cases, patients suffer from a large section of the body with scaling, scratching, and tenderness. We have a handful of moderate cases. In mild cases, large patches of the body have been reported to cause discomfort. The joints of the body are so extreme that they are swollen. Under the fingernail and the toenails, aged skin builds up. The fingernails and toenails change color, and visibility can be seen when separating from the bed.

People with this problem will see invisible signs even without medication, which means that they are still unhealed, and after a few days, symptoms appear again. Doctors will call their condition Psoriasis with a quick glance at the body covered by patches. No other tests are required, such as a blood test or urine test. By administering a few prescriptions and leading a few tips for treatment, mild cases are managed quickly. The problem will mostly be solved with medicines and recommendations for care. The same is not valid for extreme cases; they cannot be handled.

Different medications or medication combinations cannot function due to severity. There are many instances where people have been cured of homeopathic psoriasis. Homeopathy sounds pretty ideal in these days for this non-infectious health crisis. The combination of treatment and care works, however. Sunlight overexposure should be removed, the skin moisturized, smoking & alcohol gone, stress and anxiety tested and, of course, a healthy diet, all of these are included in the prescribed care tips list.

Are there any kinds?

Yes! There are several types of psoriasis: Flexural, Plaque, Guttate, Nail, Pustular, and Erythrodermic.

- The first "Plaque" is most commonly diagnosed with psoriasis among 85 % of patients, with high, inflamed, and white patches. The signs include
- "Flexural" makes the smooth skin spots, and the patients feel uncomfortable as they sweat.
- In "Guttate" cases, small circular patches over a wide area, such as arms, legs, heart, and scalp, are observed.
- "Pustular" allow the patients to suffer from high pus-filled sores. Hands and feet are the affected areas of the body.
- "Nail" affects the fingernail. It changes the look like coloring and removing the nails from the bed.

- Erythrodermic is a severe case; a wide body area is swollen. Skin will have severe swelling and dryness, causing unbearable pain in patients.

Tips for psoriasis patients

However, most medications can not permanently cure this disease since it can happen again. If it is homeopathic, a lasting cure can be expected. The correct treatment with improper care cannot improvise the condition, and proper care should also be taken. It is often advised to limit exposure to excessive heat or sunshine. Sunburns can increase pain and severity. The use of powders induces drought; the situation gets worse when the skin is dry, and this leads to itching. Hydrating the skin is essential to itching. A healthy diet should be taken with both vitamins and minerals. Perfumes should be avoided absolutely. Get plenty of water to drink and stop alcohol. The use of oatmeal baths can reduce irritation. The use of beauty products should not be made; chemicals in beauty products are not favorable for psoriasis affected by the skin. Bathing soaps should be preferred with moisturizing agents. If all of these tips are followed, the prescribed drug can function efficiently.

CHAPTER FOUR
What Are Pure Essential Oils

As the interest for people interested in alternative medicine, nutrition, and fitness increases in aromatherapy, many people ask "What are essential oils?" and "how are they different from other oils like olive oil, coconut, and the like?" This short introduction should help to clarify the subject and start in the beautiful aromatherapy world. Essential oils are condensed volatile herbal aromatic compounds-the quickly evaporated species that give plants their wonderful fragrances, which are more similar to alcohol than what we generally think of like oil.

These complex useful fluids are each derived from a specific plant species. Every plant species comes from some regions of the world, with specific environmental conditions and the fauna and flora adjacent to it. The effect is a very diverse library of aromatic compounds consisting of over 100 distinct organic chemicals, some of which are essential oils. In most plant systems, pure essential oils are distilled from oil sacs, including leaves, roots, flowers, and more. Nearly every essential oil consists of many, often hundreds of different molecular compounds. The combined compounds and their ratios give each oil its aromatic and medicinal properties.

Essential oils are not just a plant growth byproduct; plants use these oils to combat infection with bacteria, fungi, and viruses; defend themselves against animal invaders, and some suspects may be employed in chemical communication among plants of the same genus. Although the basics are from the world of plants, they are especially ideal for use in natural health, wellness, and exercise programs as they are amazingly compatible with our own chemistry. The gentlest extraction method that draws the oil from a specific plant is ideal in order to produce essential oil of therapeutic quality – those that maintain as much of the original plant essence as possible in its original condition.

Extraction methods include the extraction of carbon dioxide (CO_2) – the gentlest and most costly, pressing (as in the extraction of citrus oil from rinds) and steaming, as well as the extraction of solvents. Steam distillation is most prevalent and is regarded as gentle enough for most essential oils because it involves heating only above the boiling point. For thousands of years, human beings have used plants for healing, and from this practice, the use of aromatic plant compounds started with medicine. The recorded use of aromatic plants dates back to about 4500 B.C, but the use of oils and plant aromatics was indeed established in the hands of the ancient Egyptians. Oils have been used for embalming, medicine, and cleansing. When King Tut's tomb was opened in 1922, almost 350 liters of oil were discovered in 50 alabaster jars made. More than 200 references are made in the Old and New Testament to aromas, incense, or ointments: Frankincense, Myrrh, Galbanum, Cinnamon, Cassia, Rosemary, Hyssop, and

Spikenard are considered to be used to unite ceremonies and to cure the ill.

Modern use of essential oils in natural health, wellness, and exercise programs started in the middle of the last century with the discovery by a French scientist of Lavender's healing properties. Lavender has shown effective healing properties for skin injuries, good anti-inflammatory properties, and excellent calming effects. Further studies have confirmed that the essential oils are superior to a wide range of physiological conditions. Analysis has validated hundreds of years of practical use of essential oils, and we now know that the 'pharmacy of perfumes' includes compounds with a wide variety of biochemical effects. There are some three hundred essential oils currently being used by skilled practitioners, though 10 (for wound healing, cold-fighting, insect repelling, soothing children, etc.) could serve their average household needs, maybe 20 if their use was more esoteric (for more profound meditation, for better yoga practice).

It's effortless, enjoyable, and extremely rewarding to use essential oils. Each of these approaches is the most common application of oils: inhalation, topical application, and ingestion in certain circumstances. The diffusion of essential oils with a cold air nebulizer is better for inhalation because these oils are easily absorbed in large amounts by fine mist. This approach is useful for psychological and respiratory effects. The topical use typically involved diluting essential oils into a carrier oil at a concentration of 5% or less for some massage techniques. Massage is often used for muscle and joint pain relief as well as for psychological calming and regenerating effects. A subject is also used as mixtures to treat different diseases of the skin such as eczema, acne, and even to revitalize the aged skin. Finally, ingestion, which should only be performed with very detailed knowledge by a qualified professional, is often used as oil in gel capsules. Peppermint oil is also used in digestive conditions in this way.

There are so many wonders for essential oils that you can learn from them through courses, texts, and skilled practitioners. Be sure most of all have fun and welcome your alternative natural health, wellness, and fitness in this new version.

How to Recognize 100% Pure Essential Oils

One topic needs our full attention and is concerned with the purity of essential oils in general, and the topic of 100 % pure essential oils. This is a crucial topic because, in our time, we have problems finding pure water, pure food, and clean air, so this question of purity is also very critical in the use of natural remedies.

First of all, many believe the word "aromatherapy" refers to "healing with a strong scent," simply by re-bringing harmony into ourselves, the pleasant smell of a plant will heal. This is partially true, but not 100 % true. Let us remember that 100 % pure essential oils can be used in several ways other than through the release of fragrances and flavors, in our homes, and so on. They can also be used to massage the body and also to speed up recovery by placing them directly on the skin or injured areas. And this raises an important question: should we care for the pureness of essential oils?

And "YES" is the answer, we do. Since the active and therapeutic ingredients of all plant therapies are their natural substances, natural mother-to-nature products are perfectly balanced.

It is 100 % pure essential oils that we like. But here's the sad part, many manufacturers nowadays are not worried about the quality of their goods and the wellbeing of their consumers and want to take the short path to "success" and to their "market." Many allegedly 100 % pure oils are far from pure and far from 100%. They use phrases such as "nature-identical product," but the truth is simple: nature cannot be reproduced, it's much too complicated, and while structurally things are right, something is called "the vital force" of the plant world (which makes it heavy lifting in the healing process), which cannot be produced only in a laboratory.

Such scrupulous and irresponsible tradespeople may not know the type of harm they may do: there are allergies which, when applied to sensitive skin, can be triggered by chemical substances, and even "remedies" are sometimes induced by others instead of curing disease.

Often note that in their acts, essential oils are very reliable (because they contain naturally balanced substances): a specific part of the plant can either cure one disease or assist in a healing process (e.g., the leaves), and another can cure another (e.g., flowers). And why not, another bark will heal. The same applies to multiple families of the same species: one can actually cure while another can only rarely or never be used in aromatherapy.

The pure essential oils are somewhat specialized, and that is why one cannot merely claim to be pure: we must be sure.

Another explanation of why this has now become an issue is the issue of 'restricted capital.' More than ever, we have been aware that the resource of our world is limited and because individual plants are harvested in the wild, their use certainly has a quantitative limit. Therefore, some suppliers, aware of this issue, are trying to "pump" synthetic oils with components that are not as effective and accurate as their natural counterparts.

What to do?

Pure essence oils, usually by a method called steam distillation, are extracted from different sections of a plant or trees, but also by other ways, such as cold percolation. The methods used are mainly measures of oil purity.

Next, try to find the producer of the 100 % pure essential oil you are going to buy and do some analysis. In the world of the Internet, you can study any organization quickly nowadays. See their website, read about the manufacturing process, stocks and their management, sources of raw materials, see if there is any dispute around the particular business. Just put: be educated. Just put.

Remember these things as well:

• 100 % pure oils are usually produced in small amounts

• 100 % pure essential oils typically found in dark bottles

• 100 % pure essential oils contain no protein (these are oils), so it may very well be a sign of a synthetic drug, applied to the whole compound if you have an allergic reaction-with the exception of being a treatment for a normal vital body.

• Expense is not necessarily a quality measure. In the world of branding we live in; words are several times used irresponsibly. Brand costs. Don't take the expense as the only quality metric.

We hope that this brief advice on essential oils will help you determine how to buy essential oils, how to buy them, and how to recommend them.

And don't forget that nature is better all the time. But responsibility is crucial because nature's resources are small, and we also have to learn to give back, not just to take.

Essential Oil Safety

Essential oils are highly concentrated, particularly from the leaves, flowers, roots, and fruit of aromatic plants that come from the world of plants. While the amount of plants required producing oil varies, for example, 3.6 million- or 1000-pounds jasmine flowers are needed to produce a pound of jasmine oil. Rose oil is more concentrated, and more than 10,000 pounds of rose petals are required to produce one pound of rose oil! These two examples demonstrate both why these oils are costly and why it's so important to use them with expertise and care due to their concentrated nature.

Dilute prior to usage

Always dilute essential oils before adding them to the skin, as they can cause skin irritation, rashes, and allergic reactions if they are "neat" in their pure form. Lavender and tea tree oils are commonly listed as exceptions to this law, but diluting these oils still remains the preferred approach in most circumstances. A common rule is to add a drop of essential oil, like sweet almond or grapeseed oil, in high-quality, cold-pressed vegetable oil per teaspoon. When creating a bath with aromatherapy, add 2 to 4 drops in a warm (not hot) bath. If several oils are mixed together, treat the mixture as a single oil. In other words, use either four drops in a bath or one drop in the mix to a teaspoon of vegetable oil.

Check Patch

It is a reasonable idea to first test a patch for new flavoring oil, particularly if you have allergies or sensitive skin. Mix one drop of oil tested in a tea cubicle of base oil and dab a small amount on the inside of the arm or wrist. Wait 24 hours to ensure there is no redness or discomfort.

Matters of consistency

It is necessary to purchase high-quality oils and not to confuse essential oils with synthetic, not natural, fragrance oils. Some products marketed as pure oils are diluted or adulterated in cheaper oils. Read product labels carefully again, but know that brands may not disclose complete information. Get to know the botanical names of the oils you want to use and never buy an oil not marked by the botanical name or by the common name.

Any warnings

• Consult your doctor before using aromatherapy, whether you are pregnant or breastfeeding.

• Keep out of reach of children and pets aromatherapy products.

Keep essential oils and mucus membranes away from your eyes.

• Be very careful about furniture since undiluted oils can harm lacquered surfaces.

• The photosensitizing of citrus oils such as lemon, tangerine orange, bergamot, or grapefruit can cause sunburn. Do not use these oils in the sun or tanning beds until exposure.

• Do not use essential oils internally or under a doctor or professional practitioner's supervision. Remember that these oils are concentrated substances and, if swallowed, they may be toxic. Massage or inhalation oils are safer and extremely effective.

Aromatherapy Essential Oil Safety Tips

Aromatherapy is one of the best treatments used under the supervision of a trained doctor. Essential oils are natural plant extracts produced by steam, expression, or chemical extraction of particular plant species.

Particular attention should be paid to the application of essential oil. At some times, certain essential oils should be avoided, and other oils should be treated with caution. Some safety tips on the use of aromatherapy oils are provided here.

Be very mindful of the pure essential oil. Never put it in a pure state on your skin. Still dilute crucial oils with compact oils like almond and baby oil. If you manufacture your own oils by adding plant matter to the carrier oil, the resulting oil is weak enough to use on your skin. If you have epilepsy or allergic skin, are pregnant, are homeopathic or take another prescription drug, or have a heart condition, please contact your general health care provider before you use some essential oil. If you go out in the sun, you shouldn't add any product with citrus oils to your skin. The essential citrus oils may cause the skin to burn and redden.

Don't take essential oils by mouth. If you intend to work with oil, do a small skin test on your arm. Stop it if frustration occurs. Avoid eucalyptus, fennel, hyssop, sage, pennyroyal, juniper, tansy, thuja, tempestuous, and rosemary because of the possibility of seizures in such oils. Rosemary, wise, and thyme should be avoided by people with high blood pressure.

As an assault this may cause, asthmatics should avoid the direct inhalation of essential oils.

Stop contact with the eyes with essential oils. Essential oils are highly irritating to the eyes and should not be used close to them. Even stop rubbing your hands with the eyes that still have oil traces. You should never blaze pure oil in the oil heater and place the water in the tank and put little drop of oil to the water. It is worth noting. Keep your oils in a cool, dark place or refrigerator. Some essential organic oils are hazardous and should not be used at all, but still sold. Before you purchase, always check the safety of any oil product. Most of the time, you can confidently use widely available essential oils like lavender.

Keep essential oils out of children's control. It is safer to place it in a closed case than in a locked case. If a child ingests unintentional essential oils, don't vomit, let them drink a glass of cold water, and seek medical advice promptly and urgently.

The great advantage of aromatherapy is that most are really useful. Therapeutic herbs are those that smell healthy, so it is not too difficult to avoid those that smell bad and are potentially dangerous!

Many oils are available for children and babies under the age of 12. It is advisable to dilute with other tools these oils, which can be used for babies and young children.

Any essential oil can lead to dermatitis and sensitization, especially when repeatedly used. Stop this at any time by using only minimal quantities of gasoline. You should also practice substituting the oils from time to time instead of using the same oils every day.

When choosing essential oils, always make sure you use the correct oil by testing the Latin or botanical names. Many essential oils can have the same common name but may have numerous functions. There are also several essential oils with a familiar name.

CHAPTER FIVE
Essential Oils for Skin Care

Natural skincare products and treatments are becoming increasingly popular in society today. Beauty skincare and products encourage the use of biological and natural materials. These organic and natural ingredients and products are increasingly favored by women as we have seen the adverse effects of chemicals on our skin, body, and appearances. The next great natural skincare product is essential oils. Essential oils are removed from herbs and plants that contain the content, smell, and characteristics of the plan they have been extracted from. Essential oils in the field of skincare are pure, non-greasy oils that smell, rejuvenate, and improve the natural beauty of the skin. Essential oils can cure acne, remove scarring, lower defects, smooth wrinkles, and make signs of age disappear. Essential oils may be applied to the skin with creams, shampoos, moisturizers, lotions, or carrier oils. Evil, inflammation, psoriasis, acne, infection, sunburns, discoloration, and virtually any skin disease, problem, or discomfort that you have can be eradicated on a regular basis. A list of good essential oils for your skincare needs is given here.

Lavender-the "universal oil" is invented by Lavender because it can cure virtually every skin issue with any form of skin. It is suitable for almost everything, like relaxing, relaxing, improving mental capacity, mood, energy, etc. It has the same calming effects for the skin and treats brushes, blemishes, eczema, acne, and psoriasis. It also stimulates the growth of new cells and balances sebum production to even skin tone.

Sandalwood- Sandalwood is a highly moisturizing, dehydrated, or dry skin oil. Fine lines, scars, and wrinkles can be removed from sandalwood. It is also an antimicrobial and antibacterial agent that can reduce skin infections and acne.

Clary Sage Oil-Clary Sage is beneficial in skin issues caused by hormonal imbalances, including wrinkles, acne, and fine lines. Clary Sage has a structure identical to human hormones, so it can be used to supplement imbalanced hormones in the body if exposed. It also serves as astringent and antibacterial to destroy and cleanse infections.

Eucalyptus Oil-Eucalyptus oil is a reliable, antiseptic, antibacterial, and antiparasitic oil. It purifies the skin and eliminates skin issues, including acne, eczema, and burns. The blackheads and defects may be removed, and redness and discomfort minimized. Eucalyptus can ease uneven skin tones.

Myrrh Oil-Myrrh Oil has been used in a bazaar for centuries and, in ancient times, to treat almost every kind of illness. Chapped lips, rashes, wrinkles, defects, eczema, and bacteria have been treated in the lips.

Patchouli Oil-Patchouli oil is heavily scented and is known to treat skin disorders of all kinds. Helpful in the treatment of rashes, skin scarring, cracking and inflammation, dermatitis, acne, and eczema. It can be used to sound and tighten the skin and extract discs as a moisturizer.

How to Use Essential Oils for Skin Care?

Essential oils are available for different uses, and skincare is one of them. They are made from various plant materials, such as leaves, bulbs, roots, and barks. These goods are designed for various types of people, and so consumers need to make sure that they are picked. It is thus necessary that they learn about the various types of oils on the market to choose the one suitable for them.

To enhance the impression of a person, it is vital to take care of yourself correctly to make yourself look good. This helps to boost self-esteem by growing self-assurance that you are useful in life as you can work without difficulties through your daytime activities. One of the safest and greatest ways to do this is by using essential oils that make you smell amazing. These are mostly used in aromatherapy to open pores and to control dryness and to remove stretch marks.

There are different brands where you have the right to choose the one that best suits you for skincare. This means that when you pick the one to use, you need to be very careful to take full advantage. It is also necessary to know the outcomes to be obtained to select the best products to support. For example, a person who wishes to minimize cellulite will use items other than the one who is seeking a moisturizer. If you have a medical problem, a competent doctor should advise you in the right way.

Most essential oils are made of natural products, so people can be sure that they do not use dangerous chemicals that could cause their problems in the future. They are also easy to reach and easy to use, so you don't have to take a lot of complex procedures to make them look amazing. You can begin by using some drops of lavender, sandalwood, or rose and mix them with almond or jojoba extracts. These are really effective if you want to get dryness relief.

People may also use non-scented cream or lotion and blend it with lavender as a daily moisturizer. This is a perfect skin care technique, but you have to make sure you use high-quality items to function correctly. In this way, you don't need to struggle with flaky or ashy spots, and they will still look fantastic. These can also be used when you take a bath by adding 5-10 drops of lavender or camomile. Soak in this bath for at least a minimum of 20-30 minutes to optimum softness. This is not to be done every day as it can be done at least two or three days a week, and you will be all right.

Individuals with stretch marks should use neroli directly on problem areas. This should not be used in a sparing manner and can be diluted by the carrier. This is also a decent moisturizer and can be used every day until the desired results are achieved. You can also make a large facial toner using cedarwood and

Users should decide the purposes of choosing these items since some of them are designed for various kinds of skincare procedures. When they decide what they want to achieve, they have a simple time to choose the best product. It is also vital to note that several types of products are required to treat the bodies, such as hydrating, cleaning, and toning. Fortunately, for the various regiments that users need, several items are available.

Before choosing the best, you must consider the type of skin you have. Many with dry skins will have to pick items that are relaxed and lubricating, such as sandalwood and ylang-ylang. For those with oily ones, tea tree, lemon, and geranium products are better suited because they help to keep it dry. Some of the most common items for people dealing with acne include lemon, lavender, and tea tree, as they help avoid breakouts.

In addition to being used to hydrate, clean, and tone the body, users can also apply it to their baths. To achieve the best effect, you should fill your bathrooms and add a few drops to your product. The fundamental explanation for adding a few drops is the normal concentration of the items. They can then drink for a couple of minutes to be consumed quickly and efficiently.

The key thing that consumers must remember is to use these essential oils after diluting them. They will expose themselves to different risks if they do not dilute. The users can dilute them in a variety of ways. One of them is the use of natural carrier oils and their combination with lotions and creams to dilute them. However, care should be taken, and lanoline-free and non-scented creams should be picked. Users may also use different things like Epsom salts and oils, to make a body scrub. You are warned not to use salt scrubbing on your face because it is too rough. Users may also choose to use spritzer bottles to make a concoction of the ingredients so that they can not only cool down their bodies but also enhance their skin condition.

Best Essential Oils for Skin Care

Do we really want to look at our age, when we are thirty years old, say, above? Do we have wrinkles, fine lines, pigments, and many other side effects of aging to show the world, yes? The first indication of aging often causes a panic reaction among most of us, so it does not help to test anything available on the market. Feeling good is looking good and vice versa and looking to reverse the process? Read about some valuable tips for anti-aging skincare.

The most crucial tip for anti-aging skin care is to keep your brain healthy and trotting. Don't stay idle and think badly; play brain games; learn a new language; keep up reading, and do whatever you need to keep your brain up and running — your face is mirrored in a healthy brain. Another tip for anti-aging skincare might sound cliché, but you need plenty of fresh fruit and raw vegetables in order to be straightforward. The nutrients (vitamins, minerals, iron, anti-oxidants, etc.) you carry on the market as anti-aging skincare creams. Isn't it easier to go natural and green? At least three portions of fruits and veggies are glowing in your face every day.

Training – a must, whatever your age is. Go for morning strolls, swim, enter a gym, practice yoga at home or in a class, and you can do so many other things to move your muscles and joints. With constant exercise, your skin begins to lift and lift to give you a natural facelift without botox. Are you well and on time to sleep? The response is a simple no. Fold free when you sleep and sleep for at least 8 hours if you want your mind to work well and skin to get rid of dark under-eye circles. Note, sleep is a healthy investment in your mind and body, not a waste of time.

Yes, the sun can give you that lovely tan but think twice before you have a long exposure. Make sure you don't get out in the harsh sun for a long time, as the UV rays damage your eyes, wrinkles, and darken your skin, and can even cause cancer. Cover with a blanket and still bring sunblock lotions.

Essential Oils -A Beginners Guide to Better Health Through Ancient Practices

Diet is an immense problem for many people today who either want to suppress a preventable illness or is attempting to lose their extra weight. Our diet is not only getting worse as Americans but as our population has increased, there have been very few efforts to address the harmful effects of our food production. Every single American who has eaten the hot lunches in school recalls the taste of the preservatives and created the taste of the food they ate during the primary education years.

To understand our diet, we need to look at what has been around for centuries—actually, at least two generations. The only generation that did not see food processed and packed for "shelf life" in its entirety was our best generation ... Those people who fought and won the Second World War, many exposed to it in the military during their days, but probably had grown much of their food by themselves up until then or had at least access to new, foods without preservatives. What was the timeline that has triggered the most significant shortage of fundamental components that food has ever experienced?

You, like me, went to the supermarket and purchased a cereal box and a bag of flour, rice, or other grain of canned vegetables to see on the side or labels the words 'enriched' or 'fortified.' What do these words mean? What do these words mean? Why does food need to be enriched or strengthened? The answer is so simple that the next time you go shopping, you start seeing it everywhere! It'll be at least an item that you bring home from the store, and you might be fortunate to come home with something that is neither fortified nor enhanced, depending on how you do it. They have to be enriched and improved since they are extracted and altered until they are shelved in your local supermarket.

As a result of this method of de-fooding vital nutrients, minerals, and compounds, every American knows that we have to take a "healthy vitamin supplement." So many people out there are that it is confusing to decide which are useful to improve our own diets. It's a small effort since the bulk of the multi-vitamins we use are processed through our digestive tract with limited intestinal absorption.

The worst thing to come is our well-being and safety if the way our food is delivered and processed can't or can't improve. What other essential ingredients, apart from the vitamins and minerals we don't substitute every day? Can the negative effects of our over processed, fast-run, canned, improved, and enriched source of food be countered? The response is a loud YES!

Unfortunately, once our food is eliminated, it is usually permanent. We can not take the same constituents that make up our fruits and vegetables or herbs and replenish them so that they have the exact chemical machining and benefit to us when we eat them. There are now substances reintroduced that are essential oils as one of the most beneficial substances removed in the production of our foods.

Essential oil is the nature of the plant, and it never comes from an animal source. This does not mean that we are in favor of vegetarianism or veganism, as this is a particular preference for your own dietary requirements and choices. But essential oils are a good way to complement what vegetarians and vegans have to eat without increasing all their food, but we are digressed. Essential oils belong to the Alternative Medicine group but are increasingly important in traditional medicine because scientists are aware, because of the wide variety of components, of the importance of these fundamental substances.

The essential oils are the natural aromatic compounds found from bark to roots to flowers in the various parts of the plant. They can be stunning and heavily scented. Take the leaf of any fresh herb such as thyme or coriander to verify this, and rub the leaves in your hands. Take a deep breath, and the essential oils will smell. Whether you've appreciated the gift of a rose, a field of lavender, or the new scent of cut mint, you've come across the aromatic qualities of essential oils. Essential oils are ten times stronger and better than their dried herbal equivalents, mostly sprinkled and distilled for the sake of foods and aromas. These essential oils give the plants a distinctive scent but also protect them against predators and help pollinate them.

Essential oils are non-water-based organic compound phytochemicals. While fat-soluble, or the acids found in animal oils or vegetable are not included. Essential oils are almost crisp to the touch, very clean and immediately absorbed by the skin. You can never leave an oily mark or feel on your skin when it is in its purest state. The essential pure, unadulterated oils are pellucid and have a clear blue hue.

Over and beyond their inherent benefits to plants and exquisite scents of humans, essential oils have been used for their medicinal and therapeutic use in many cultures throughout history. Modern scientific research and trends towards more holistic health approaches revitalize and rediscover essential applications in oil health. The Egyptians were among the first people in medical practice, beauty treatment, food preparation, and a religious celebration to use aromatic essential oils extensively.

Besides its source, the same oils mentioned above are still used in Middle Eastern cultures to avoid common infant and child illnesses; that in the Western world, when we or our children get sick, we are inoculated or some kind of prescription medication. Is it any wonder that two of the items which are now scientifically investigated in essential oils were at the foot of Jesus Christ while he was lying in a manger?

In modern times, the powerful curative properties of essential oils in 1937 and healed a badly burnt hand with pure lavender oil. A French contemporary used essential medicinal oil for the care of wounded soldiers during the Second World War. Since the Second World War, the modern use of essential oils has continued to develop rapidly as health scientists, alternative, and traditional phytosanitary practitioners continue to explore and verify the various health and wellness benefits of essential oils.

"Essential oils are used for a wide variety of mental and physical health uses. They are appropriate as one oil at a time or in complex blends depending on consumer experience and desired value. It is important that you consult an expert in essential oil discipline before starting an active diet.

Our sense of smell influences many pathways of physiology, including hormone stimulation and other metabolic processes. Aromatherapy is based on the predictable body response to such olfactory stimuli. Essential oils are commonly used in applications of aromatherapy. Certain essential oils can be very stimulating when diffused in the air while others can be calming and soothing. In addition to emotional benefits, spreading essential oils will purify the air from unnecessary fragrances produced by pets or extracted from tobacco and certain airborne pathogens. Important oil diffusers with low to no heat are recommended as they do not alter the chemical composition of the oil that is being diffused. Essential oils can also be used in the house as purification and purification additives for washing machines and surface cleaners.

Given the ability of our senses to directly affect our hormone balance and other body functions, stimuli that can help keep the balance in our bodies are important and necessary. It is not shocking that many of us today experience the effects of all the human chemicals stored and constructed in our bodies by inhalation or intake, which we still have with us.

We all eat processed foods that are good only as empty calories if we are fortunate. Then when we lack energy, we add the lack of energy from these fatty, expensive bouffs of nothingness to energy drinks, which are so full of chemical stimulants that you expect to have a proverbial "popeye moment" of spinach and spring in motion with nothing but the villainy that you personally face with a quick combination. The truth is this, the results usually are shakes or jitters that precede a crash leaving the rest of the day missing. Like all stimulants, you will eventually have to increase the dosage to obtain the same results. All this is because we, as Americans, have decided we want "bigger, stronger, quicker, more," and we want this yesterday! We must start to "decide" and choose to regain control over all aspects of our health.

You just need to discover the world of certified pure therapeutic grade essential oil in order to re-equilibrate your body and restore the natural energy from a food source.

CHAPTER SIX
Organic Essential Oil

Do you really try to suggest that there is a big difference between traditional essential oil and essential organic oil? This question is amazing, so let's get to it? No exception to certified organic herbal oil is the aromatherapy buff. Organic oil really isn't produced in a science laboratory-like many industrial herbal oils that you find. It's organic. The hard chemicals you find in the counterpart are not an important one. Think about what we do with these oils? We breathe it and place it on our skin. Do you really want anything to be made of chemicals from a laboratory into you?

We would also like to emphasize that organic essential oils are excellent for the climate, considering the emphasis on the green movement. While herbal oils are natural, it is important to dilute them before applying them. If you massage aromatherapy, you really want to ensure that it dilutes with what the industry calls carrier oils. Either canola or olive oil should blend organically essential oils to minimize aromatherapy. If you use organic essential oil in your bath, then you really don't have to worry because you just put concentrated oil in your bath between 10-20 drops in anywhere, and you are good to go. Aromatherapy is an ancient science that is much older, and my personal conviction is that you have to use the components that are closest to nature. That is indeed the essence of aromatherapy, and we think you are separating art from science with synthetic herbal oils if that makes sense.

Ordinarily, aromatherapy experts will agree that placing some herbal oils alone on the skin is a bad idea, whether their synthetic or organic herbal oils are a bad idea. Human skin is not ready to consume something of this nature even if that's real; we still want pure organic essential oils in our skin even if it's diluted in the chemical. You can easily overdo the amount of organic essential oil you use so that you still extract the oils, however. When you shop for organic oil, it is vital that you understand what you pay for. The cheapest herbal oil is synthetic for the saved time. Even when you buy organic essential oil, you know that even though it costs a little extra, it will pay off for the gain. The best is organic oil! Organic oil!

Certified Organic Essential Oil and Its Uses

Experts claim that, compared to the essential oils developed in these laboratories, pure organic essential oils are milder and do not contain harmful chemicals that can cause health problems. In addition, certified organic essential oils consist of natural ingredients and are entirely environmentally-friendly and biodegradable.

There are many applications of certified organic essential oil. This sort of oil you can use for your bath, perfume, personal care, and massage oil. For several years, the use of this oil has been related to wellness and good health. Research shows that people who use organic essential oil are less likely than people who do not have this type of treatment at home to certain types of disorders. If you want to enjoy your well-being entirely, you should stop using conventionally manufactured oils and turn to organic oils.

For various years people from all over the world have used oil in their bathrooms. Long before they became permanent establishments in wellness centers & spas, these kinds of oil were the favorite royalty bathing oils.

You simply add about 10-20 concentrated drops in your hot bath to use certified organic essential oil in your bath. When you use diluted versions, at least a cup of it should be added to your water.

Diluted oil is vital for your message. No, you shouldn't try to add pure necessary directly to your skin. Experts claim they can be too intense for most skin types and can cause irritation. In order to prevent unwanted injuries, blend your oils with carrier oils to make your skin more comfortable. Canola oil, mineral oil, olive oil, and almond oil are some of the most familiar carrier oils you can use along with your certified organic essentials.

Essential oils can be used for the treatment of hair and skin. You should consider using certified organic, essential oil on your hair if you have dry hair and scalp itches. Add diluted essential oil to your bath for dry skin or apply it with a sponge while taking a shower.

The Basics of Organic Essential Oils

Essential oils are concentrated fluids extracted from plants and are very popular in therapeutic applications. Essential oils have many components, and each of them has a number of health benefits. Among essential oils, organic essential oils are considered superior. The origins of these oils are plants grown on land approved by an accredited regulatory agent without the use of any fertilizers, pesticides, or harmful chemicals. They are considered organic only if the plant from which it is extracted is grown using environmentally friendly methods in good soil.

Bio essential oil becomes very popular among nurses and aromatherapists who prefer to use it in clinical treatments. In contrast to traditional essential oils, these oils have more potency and healing properties. If you take pesticide residues into account, organic oils are suitable not just for the environment but also for human bodies. Certified dealers in these oils ensure that consumers obtain goods that are analytically checked and certified in one of the following official regulatory bodies:

• Nature and Progress

• ECOCERT

• Agrobio

• The Association of Soil

• Qualite-France SA

A number of organizations insure organic plants and organic essential oils and thereby ensure that the oil that you purchase is approved and expected to benefit from therapy. These oils are much superior in terms of fragrance. This is because they are more centered than ordinary oils. In addition to the scent, they also have good taste, since they are also used for cooking.

A variety of balanced, flavored dishes can be made with organic essential oils. Oils such as organic basil oil have a more appetizing flavor compared to the dried and fresh herbs used to cook. They do not contain a molecule of glycerol that makes tongue fatty oils fatty. This makes them better than fatty oils such as sesame or olive oil. Natural oils have antiseptic, antiviral, and antibacterial elements in place of fat. You can bathe and rub any of these oils on your skin. Her steam can also be inhaled for some medicinal effects. As they are more advantageous and superior, they are bound to be more costly than any other essential oil. The ones harvested in the wild are even more costly.

Today you will find many vendors selling organic essential oils, but they do not meet all of the criteria of an 'organic' product. Make sure you purchase items that have an 'organic' label. Many well-known suppliers mark items with common botanical names, a part of the plant used, the country of origin, the oil extraction method, and the agriculture method. If all of this information is not part of any packet of essential oils, it is advised not to use these oils as they can adversely affect your body.

Use Organic Essential Oils for Massage and Aromatherapy

The pure extracts of plants that give the full fragrance and taste of the plant are organic essential oils. Natural essential oils, depending on the plant variety, can be taken from the flora, leaf, fruit, seed, root, or bark of the plant. Concentrated oils for massage and aromatherapy are used.

Massage Oils

The essential organic oils, like crucial organic lavender oil, are suitable for scenting oils used for massage therapies. Since they are so concentrated, most organic essential oils should be diluted with carrier oils, such as almond oil or olive oil, for healthy use in the skin.

It takes only a few drops of essential organic lavender oil to perfume your massage oil. After it has been added, the comforting and relaxing aroma of lavender will scent your skin. Organic lavender essential oil or other oil scents massage oils allow your hands to move over the skin effortlessly, making tightened muscles easier to massage and relieve the kinks. The organic lavender essential oil can be applied as an aroma to the body lotions as body soaks for use in the bath for a soothing scented bath in conjunction with the carrier oils.

Aromatherapy Oils

Aromatherapy oils can be used to improve your mood and make the air around you a good fragrance. Aromatherapy oils, including essential organic lavender oil, are dispersed across the air throughout the room using a diffuser.

Different kinds of diffusers are used for several purposes. The smallest ones are personal diffusers and automotive diffusers. Personal diffusers are small bottles with a few drop of aromatherapy oil inside that is used to disperse the fragrance around the neck and body heat. Car diffusers are small containers with the essential oil that can be hanging from the mirror or bung into the cigarette lighter in your car.

Organic essential lavender oil can also be used for diffusers that smell your room. You may use a candle, a lightbulb, or power to heat the essential oils. Lightbulb rings are very user friendly. On top of a bulb in the lamp, you simply place a metal or ceramic hole ring, add a few drops of oil in the ring, and then turn on the light. The heat extracts the scent from the bulb. Candle diffusers offer an oil basin with a heat source candle below. Electric diffusers are useful to perfume a whole room and are also provided by small fans to spread the fragrance.

Natural essential oils are suitable for use in massage and aromatherapy applications in all these respects.

Are Organic Essential Oils Really Organic?

Many companies today claim to supply products that offer 'organic essential oils.' However, several companies sell organic products that are not USDA certified but nevertheless say that they are on product labels. In order for a company to legally describe its goods as organic, it must follow USDA requirements. However, the USDA does not yet have the most challenging requirements to follow, as other requirements such as CCOF International and IFOAM also have more rigorous criteria to fulfill to be accredited.

What is certification?

If a company is certified that the products are genuinely organic, then this ensures that the oils are derived from plants and that no additives are used.

For example, conventional methods of farming also require the use of chemical pesticides and other associated products, but plants designated for the production of organic essential oils cannot be administered. This implies, of course, that chemical compounds cannot even be used to treat the soil of these plants. In addition, if chemicals have been used in soil, it must take a certain period of time before the soil is used for the cultivation of organic plants to ensure that no residue is left.

Why is organic more expensive?

Organic companies use pesticides and natural fertilizers to grow their plants rather than to use chemicals to produce rich plants. However, more resources, time, and money are needed to use these natural methods when making organic oils.

Consequently, organic essential oils are more high cost than traditional oils, such as organic but not certified oils. You can see, however, why companies try to get organic when they don't really. They want to save money, although they can still enter this target market.

Health advantages

In any event, people eating food or using products made of these plants can have these chemicals passed on to them because plants and soil can absorb chemicals that were applied to them. This is why it is important to use organic essential oils.

The fruit trees sprayed with pesticides from which some essential oils are extracted have fruits that absorb the pesticide and are therefore polluted. Organic essential oils avoid being contaminated, as these companies do not use harmful chemicals.

CONCLUSION

Therapy of massage oil based on the use of essential (concentrated) plant oils heals pain. The oils are generally massaged into the skin, placed in a bath, or inhaled. Unlike herbal medicinal products, oils are not concentrated from whole plant portion but are usually extracted from leaves, flowers, grasses, roots, peel, resin, or bark by steam distillation.

Essential oil is now used to treat a variety of conditions and is supposed to work physically and psychologically with people. The first part of the theory is that when you smell an essential oil, it activates your limbic system-the part of the brain that regulates emotions and stores and retrieves acquired memories-and relaxes you. The other part of the theory is that the essential oils are absorbed into the skin and have medicinal properties that are responsible for the problem.

Some of the essential oil conditions for treatment include anxiety, insomnia or stress, menopausal or menstrual problems, headaches, eczema, pains and muscular aches, digestive problems, asthma.

You can look for an aromatherapist or purchase those essential oils in a counter and treat yourself in pharmacy and health stores. They are used as massage oils, applied to the bath, or inhaled with steaming water, an incense or a diffuser.

Some products such as aromatherapy products contain only small amounts of essential oils. But the oils can be very powerful in their concentrated form and should be carefully handled-just a few drops are needed in a bath. More of it may cause discomfort and when used improperly. Essential oils may have side effects – for example, headaches, nausea or an allergic reaction. Some react with ultraviolet light, like citrus oils e.g. peach, citrus, and bergamot, and can make the skin more easily burn in the sunlight.

CPSIA information can be obtained
at www.ICGtesting.com
Printed in the USA
LVHW051048241220
675071LV00003B/498

9 781801 445795